THE

BUSINESS OF

CO-PARENTING

For Stepparents

**How to Responsibly Invest in
Your Blended Family
&
Build Harmony**

MERISSA V. GRAYSON, ESQ.

MVG Publishing c/o Merissa V. Grayson, 21151 S. Western Ave, Torrance, CA 90501

Ordering Information:
Quantity sales. Special discounts are available on quantity purchases by corporations, associations, and others. For details, contact the publisher at the address above.
Orders by U.S. trade bookstores and wholesalers. Please contact info@americasblendedfamilyexpert.com

Library of Congress Cataloging-in-Publication Data

Merissa V. Grayson, Esq.
The Business of Co-Parenting for Stepparents: How to Responsibly Invest in Your Blended Family & Build Harmony.
Edited by: Ebony Finley
Published By: MVG Publishing

Printed in the United States of America

Disclaimer: This book is intended only as an informative guide for those seeking tips for better co-parenting. This book is for informational purposes only and based on California law. The suggestions and strategies contained herein may not be suitable for your situation. You should consult with a professional therapist, coach, or attorney independently where appropriate, as neither the publisher nor the author will assume responsibility for any consequences of actions taken based upon the information herein. Although the author made efforts to provide quality information, the author does not make any promises, claims, or guarantees about the adequacy, or completeness of the information. As legal advice must be specifically tailored to the facts and circumstances of each case, the legal information contained herein is for informational purposes only and does not constitute legal advice. It is neither intended to create nor does create an attorney-client relationship. Should you need legal advice, you should consult with an attorney independently.

Dedication

For my ~~Step~~dad, who taught me that parenthood is not defined by your DNA, but by making the <u>choice</u> to love a child unconditionally as your own, when you don't have to.

CONTENTS

Preface

Today, I am a Child Custody Attorney, Mediator, and Co-Parent Coach. I've been referred to as "America's Blended Family Expert" in part because of the work that I do in helping parents learn to co-parent successfully. But, it seems like just yesterday that my family fit the profile of a reality tv show. Move over "The Real housewives" and "Love & Hip Hop."

The ironic thing about my story is that if you had asked me if I would ever marry someone with children, my answer would have been "absolutely not." In fact, I'd sworn that I wouldn't even date a man with children because I didn't want to deal with the drama that typically comes with that territory. Then, I met my now husband who had a son from a previous relationship and that's when the drama (you know…the drama I planned to avoid by not dating a man with kids) began. We've been through it all: fights, an intense custody battle, restraining orders, jail, police intervention, sadness, anger, frustrations, confusion and eventually understanding, appreciation, happiness… and *finally* peace. You might be reading this thinking that your situation is too far gone, and I remember feeling the same way. However, after years of trial and error, and learning some valuable lessons, our lives changed for the better and we created what feels like magic; two separate homes filled with harmony, peace and love.

Years later, when I opened my family law practice, I began to notice a recurring trend in the families I worked with. It seemed that even after my clients' legal issues were resolved, the struggle to co-parent cooperatively remained. Getting a legal "order" did nothing to change the day-to-day conflict or drama that their families faced. Their lives seemed to mirror the life I had prior to figuring out how to resolve my own co-parenting issues. So, I started working with my clients, sharing some of the strategies my family implemented and encouraging them to make a positive shift in the way they think and co-parent. As a result, many have achieved a level of peace that custody orders alone do not afford.

The Business of Co-Parenting series was inspired after looking back on my journey and realizing not only how drastically my family's life had changed for the better, but also the overwhelming positive changes in my clients' lives when we worked together to implement the same strategies that worked for my family. The series is 3-part and of course features a title for moms and dads, but I was sure to include a third title for stepparents not only because I have first-hand knowledge and experience in this arena, but also because I now understand that a stepparent's role is just as significant as mom's and dad's. Although often overlooked, your actions, including the support you give (or withhold from) your spouse, the bond you develop with your stepchild, as well as your relationship (or lack thereof) with the other parent, has an incredible impact on what that child's life will be like. It is my hope that by learning and implementing the strategies discussed in this book, your family won't have to go through what my family went through. But, if you're already going through it, it is also my hope that like my situation, your situation can drastically improve and you can experience the co-parenting peace you deserve.

Sincerely,

Merissa V. Grayson

Introduction

Life changes the moment you decide that you are going to marry the love of your life. But, when you decide to marry the love of your life who also happens to have a child (or children) from a previous relationship, life changes on a "whole 'nother level." Not only do you make a transition from dating to marriage (which is a journey in of itself), but you are also taking on the responsibility that many simply cannot handle - being a stepparent. According to the United States Census Bureau:

-40% of couples that live together have children in the home;

-Approximately 68% of remarriages involve children;

-1 out of 3 people have a stepparent, stepchild, or stepsibling; and

-2,000 new blended families are formed every day.

The unfortunate thing about these statistics, is that based on years of studies, there's an unwavering consensus that children in blended families face greater negative risks than their counterparts. They face an increased risk of conflict in the home, are three times more likely to need psychological counseling, and are more likely to drop out of school, abuse drugs and alcohol, have greater and earlier sexual activity, experience incarceration and experience teenage pregnancy. Let's face it…when you look at the stats, the odds are definitely not in a blended family's favor. But why? We know that there are many successful blended families all around the world who never fall within the realm of these statistics. So, what is it that sets these blended families apart from those who are ill-fated? I believe it all has to do with the family dynamic as a whole – the mindset, attitudes, actions, and relationships of the parents, stepparents, and children involved. And it may surprise you to learn that you have more influence on the above than you may realize.

This book is all about defeating the odds of those negative statistics that target both your marriage and your stepchildren by implementing a concept I like to call "The Business of Co-Parenting.

"The Business of Co-Parenting" Explained

❖ *Co-Parenting Defined*

Co-parenting is a relationship between parents who are not married, living together or otherwise in an intimate relationship, yet they *work together* with one another to organize their child's daily life and activities to ensure that the child receives the most consistent lifestyle and discipline possible and to ensure that each parent is fully aware of and involved in all issues related to their child. Essentially, the goal is to ensure that the parents and the child are all on the same page, and function as one family unit despite being divided into two separate homes.

I've learned through trial and error that a large part of successful blended family living is based upon your mindset and how you handle different situations. Although all divided/blended families have different issues and experiences, I've discovered that the most successful way to make headway towards harmonious blended family living is to manage it as if you were managing a business. Most established businesses have designated high-ranking officers such as the CEO/President, Vice President, etc. These individuals are typically in charge of total management and control of the business and act as a leader, director, and decision-maker. In the "Co-Parenting Business," these roles are likely held by your spouse and your stepchild's other parent. Other critical components to a successful business are shareholders and investors. Shareholders are a company's owners. They have the potential to profit if the company does well, but that comes with the potential to lose if the company does poorly. According to the dictionary, an investor essentially "uses, gives, or devotes (time, talent, etc.), for a purpose or to achieve something." That's where you come in. As the new member of this now blended family, you essentially become a "shareholder/investor" of this "co-parent business." Your role is now much more than an outsider of no importance; you are now an owner of this business, charged with the role of devoting your support, time, and life to your spouse and stepchildren.

In order to master the business of co-parenting, you must first and foremost *own* your position. Using the tips in this book, you will learn to *responsibly* invest in your blended family and build the harmony needed for your family to thwart those negative statistics previously mentioned. You will learn how to use your objective perspective to support your spouse in taking control of negative or taxing co-parenting situations and redirect them into a markedly more positive direction. Equally important, you will learn how to establish and handle your relationships with your stepchild and their other parent. By taking the business-approach as opposed to an emotional-approach, you will clearly focus on the task at hand - to protect the most important assets of your business, your marriage and your stepchildren. By maintaining a business model mindset, you will communicate clearly and directly, be proactive and avoid problems. At the same time, when problems or disagreements arise - which unfortunately are oftentimes unavoidable - you will have the tools to effectively resolve or minimize them.

❖ *The "Business" Perspective*

Let me put things into a more clear perspective for you:

Imagine that at your current job (or in your current business) there's a two billion dollar business opportunity for you (a legal one that doesn't go against your personal morals of course); let's say, a "promotion" or "bonus." In order for you to obtain this bonus or promotion, the only thing you would have to do is perform your usual job duties while working with an assigned team and manager, and show that you're a good "team player." That sounds reasonable right? I mean, regardless of your current financial situation right now, I'm sure you could use an additional two billion dollars. I'm also sure, that if the possibility of this two billion dollar promotion or bonus were on the table in real life, you would do <u>whatever</u>, literally (within reason of course) to protect this two billion dollar deal and make sure it didn't fail. You would more than likely deal with ugly attitudes, extra-long hours, being overworked, excessive criticism, picking up the slack of lazy or incompetent team members or ungrateful managers, and much more, as long as at the end of the project, you were going to get paid. Ironically, you've probably already dealt with these types of things in your current or previous job just to ensure that you would remain employed, and could make just enough to pay your bills or live paycheck to paycheck.

I hope that you would agree that your stepchild and the success of your blended family are worth much more than two billion dollars. So, considering what you've already dealt with in order to maintain something that is of no comparison when it comes to true value, ponder this: Your spouse and your stepchild's other parent are your assigned team-members and/or managers. <u>Your blended family is that two billion dollar business deal</u>. **What are you willing to do to protect it and ensure its success?** From this point forward, this is the mindset you must maintain in order to master The Business of Co-Parenting; dealing with your blended family relationships like a business investment, with a very valuable deal on the line. You will be proactive, communicate with your spouse, stepchild, and their other parent clearly and directly without sweating the small stuff, and will as a result be able to protect your family's interests by lessening the potential for drama and chaos.

I.

BLENDED FAMILY DYNAMICS

To build harmony in your blended family, you must first develop realistic expectations, understand your role as a stepparent, and responsibly invest in your blended family accordingly.

Stepping In: Welcome to the Family

The fact is, although your spouse and stepchild's other parent are no longer in a romantic or intimate relationship, they are still a family. Their DNA chains have been joined to create your stepchild who is a part of both of them. Whether they or you like it or not, they are eternally tied together, as their child now has family that stems from both of them. And now *you* are added to that same family tie. You are now part of a blended family unit that must peacefully work together until your stepchild reaches 18 years old, and perhaps beyond.

Successful blended family living is definitely a skill to be mastered; it requires consistent dedication, understanding, compromise, and a level of *maturity* that many people are incapable of obtaining due to stubbornness, ignorance, or just plain old stupidity;

that's why you hear more "horror" stories about stepparents and stepchildren rather than those that mirror the Brady Bunch. Hopefully you won't have that problem. You can tackle this, no problem. You *will* tackle this for your spouse, stepchild, and for your own sanity. *By* reading this book you have taken a major step. You will master what I like to call, as mentioned in the Introduction, The Business of Co-Parenting - a method for co-parenting without the unnecessary drama. It all starts with your mindset. And believe it or not, it's one of the best gifts you can give to your family.

What to expect - Blended Family Territory

Although no blended family is the same, many have a lot of the same common experiences. There are some things that naturally come with the territory of blended family living. At first, I stepped into my blended family with no idea about what to expect. I took my family for what it was. I didn't understand the dynamics of everyone involved. I didn't understand that when you make the decision to marry someone with children from a previous relationship that you are transitioning into a blended family derived from brokenness. I know, that doesn't sound too pretty, but the reality is, when you blend a family, things don't always look or sound pretty.

Think about it like this: when you blend several different ingredients together, is it always pretty? Absolutely not. Sometimes the outcome is something that looks pretty, but tastes awful. Other times, the final product doesn't look appealing at all, but turns out to be the best green smoothie you've ever had. It all depends on what different ingredients are put into the blender and how they interact with each other. A blended family is no different, sometimes you may have it all together and blend with ease. Other times things won't be so pretty; it all depends on what you put into it.

Marjorie Howard said it best when she said "in a blended family, everyone is broken." It's true. If you think about it, there aren't too many people who would choose to have a child with someone and the relationship with that person not work out. Most people would not list "becoming a single parent" as one of their lifetime goals. And no child wants to grow up daddy-less, mother-less, or with separated parents. With that in mind, it's important to understand that when you marry your spouse, you are essentially stepping into a place of brokenness and loss– lost relationships, lost friendships, lost love, lost trust, lost patience, lost pride, lost stability, lost peace, and so much more. With that territory often comes a lot of emotions, ill feelings, and even drama. So, where exactly do you fit in here? How are you going to step into this new place without committing to a life of drama? The answer to this question is: by responsibly investing in your blended family and building a life of harmony.

Responsible Investing Explained:

Another thing I've learned about stepparenting is the importance of our role as a stepparent. As stepparents, we step into our blended family not knowing the exact circumstances that have taken place between our spouses, their children, and the other parent prior to our arrival. We learn what we think we need to know about our new family from our spouse and we naturally tend to take everything our spouses tell us about their past, their ex, their children, and their relationships (or lack thereof) at face value. We do so without considering other perspectives, and before we have had the chance to fully assess the situation, we have made a decision that is fully aligned with our spouse's perspective and that may not always be fitting. You know, he said his ex is "crazy" so you assume this is true. She said her ex is a jerk, so you deal with him accordingly. We do this all in the name of "supporting our spouse." Most married people will tell you that they will go to bat for their spouse no matter what. It doesn't matter how right or wrong they are; most people naturally want to support their spouse in everything they do. You are essentially entering into a life-long partnership with your spouse – a commitment. I completely understand and agree that supporting your spouse is absolutely necessary. At the same time, you must remember too that it's no longer just about you and your spouse. The support you lend must be for the best interest of your *entire* blended family in mind; failing to do this will likely lead to thoughtless decisions that may have a detrimental impact on everyone involved.

Responsibly investing means being supportive but more importantly it means not being <u>blindly</u> supportive of your spouse without considering whether they are right, wrong, or if there may be a better way. Responsibly investing means investing yourself as if this is your family...because in actuality, now it is.

I learned this lesson the hard way; that's one of the things that inspired me to write this book. When I was dating my husband, I just took things for what they were. I was with my husband, he had a child, his child had a mom, and that was that. Other than taking his side, I didn't really voice an independent opinion. I didn't really care about how anyone else felt about the fact that my husband and I were together or how it may have affected them. As long as you didn't bother me, I didn't bother you. When conflict arose, I "wasn't in it," (and if I was, I was unequivocally in accord with him without consideration of everything or everyone else). I later learned that was a terrible attitude to have. When you're in a blended family, you don't really have the option to not be "in it." You're in it, right smack dab in the middle of "it." - whatever "it" is, whether indirectly or directly and whether you want to be or not.

What I also realized is that in a blended family, as a stepparent, you are really the only one with an objective perspective; you're the only one who had no involvement in the relationship between your spouse and your child's other parent. Considering this, there may be many times where your thoughts and input may be the only rational one available and how you support your spouse, engage with your stepchild, and interact with the other parent will greatly influence the direction in which your family is headed.

Know your role:

Blended family life is challenging. Not everyone can do it. I suppose that explains why approximately 60% of 2nd and 3rd marriages that end in divorce cite children as being the cause. Not only does your life change when you marry someone with children, but when you step into the picture, the dynamic of what your spouse, their child, and their child's other parent is accustomed to will also go through a major transition. This family has already had to adjust to the end of the intimate relationship between your spouse and your stepchild's other parent. Additionally, they may have also had to adjust to moving into separate homes and possibly complete lifestyle shifts. Now, they must adjust to a new person joining their family whether they were ready or not and irrespective of what they may be individually dealing with. For this reason, from the moment you committed to your spouse, your role became significant - likely more significant than you may have realized.

The reality is, you don't have just one role. Because there are several relationship components in a blended family, you will naturally assume multiple roles. At first it may feel overwhelming to find your place - your sweet spot where you feel comfortable with everyone involved. This is especially true if your spouse and their child's other parent have had a tumultuous relationship and have not yet reached a place of peace and cooperation. But once you learn to appreciate the significance of your roles, you'll understand the positive impact your actions alone can have on your family and you'll find it easier to get there.

❖ *The Neutral*

Because you are a new facet of this family, you have the unique opportunity to assume a neutral position. You haven't been involved in much of the happenings of the past that are related to the dynamics of your blended family, specifically the things that may have caused strain between your spouse and stepchild's other parent, or even your stepchild. Keeping this in mind, it's important to consider all situations that come up in your blended family from a place of neutrality. Without making an allowance for any preconceived notions you may have about everyone involved based on what you "know" about the past, start from the middle of the road, remaining as impartial as possible. Essentially, regardless of what has happened in the past between your spouse, the other parent, and your stepchild, in your mind, give everyone a fresh start- a clean slate and encourage everyone else to do the same. It may be difficult for everyone else to do at the outset, as they are all likely mired by things that have happened between them in the past. But, your neutral position can help everyone through this. Now, I'm not saying that you should *agree* with everyone for the sake of not taking sides. In fact, your perspective will be important in a lot of situations. But, by starting from a neutral place before arriving at or expressing a particular point of view and by remaining neutral when discussing important thoughts, feelings, and making decisions related to your blended family, you can lead your family to a place that's less driven by the past and guided more with the future in mind. "You'll never get to the destination you're trying to reach if you constantly travel back down the road you're trying to leave." Your neutral perspective will remind everyone to consider how this will affect everyone involved.

❖ *The Leader*

Because you are one of the newest members of your blended family, you may be tempted to simply fall in line with the way things are already working in your family. And, if things are going smoothly, that is a good idea. You know the saying: "If it isn't broken, don't try to fix it." But, as previously mentioned, when you're in a blended family, not only is everyone involved likely broken in some way, but everything may also be broken, including the way things are working. Although you may not be acting as the CEO or Partner in this business of co-parenting, the reality is, this is your family too now. You are an investor in this business and as a responsible investor, you have to know when to take the lead if necessary. I don't mean take control of everything and start calling the shots. What I mean is, in all that you do, lead by example; your actions will have a great impact on the way things go in your family. The fact is: No matter how influential you are, you can't make people change. People change when THEY decide and the best way to foster harmony in your blended family relationships is to model the behavior that you wish to see in everyone else. It starts with you. You can influence others to want to change by being an example.

11

If you want someone to do something right, do a great job at showing them how it's done.

❖ *The Supporter*

You are probably your spouse's biggest supporter. If you're not, you should be. When it comes to blended family living, your spouse will rely on your support more than anyone else's; you're the one they're closest to everyday and who will witness all of the emotions that come with the territory of blended family living. This includes the frustration, anger, sadness, fear, confusion, happiness, love, and so much more. You are their "better half." Sometimes, they'll need you to simply be a sounding board. Sometimes, they'll need you to be their voice of reason. Sometimes they'll need a hug and a shoulder to lean on. You will be their confidant, their cheerleader, and likely their best friend. You absolutely should be all of these things for your spouse. Just remember to responsibly support them (as discussed above). As their biggest supporter, you are there to not only encourage them, but to listen to them and help them with their challenges. In order to do that for their benefit, you must be objective and honest in your support.

❖ *The Bonus Parent*

A stepparent's role, albeit very different, is just as significant as mom's and dad's. Everything you say and/or do can greatly impact your stepchild's life. You've essentially inherited a bonus child and they've inherited a bonus parent. Though many children have two parents, your stepchild has the privilege of having three (and in some cases 4). This means that you must conduct yourself accordingly. Just like their biological parents, you are not there to be their "friend." You are a trusted adult who at times will be required to give parental advice, make parental decisions, give parental support, offer parental protections and deal with parental problems.

❖ *The Peacekeeper*

Peace is one of the most important things in life. When you're at peace with yourself, your circumstances, and the people around you, everything in life becomes so much easier. So, my philosophy is, if you want peace in your home, then you must be the peacekeeper. As the peacekeeper, you can ensure that all issues that come up in your family are handled with care. I encourage having a "no drama" policy. By enforcing this rule, you not only protect your own peace, but you also create an environment of peace for your family. As soon as situations head in the direction of drama, encourage the opposite. When you see things escalating, help tone it down. Encourage the cooperation and compromise that will be necessary to make things work. As the peacekeeper, it's your job to remind everyone that disagreement is okay, but disrespect is not, civil discussions are okay, but arguments without boundaries are not. As the only member of your blended family that doesn't have any pre-conceived "drama" with everyone else involved, this is a role that is easiest for you to assume because you have an objective perspective. You can bring an entire new realm of positive energy to your blended family that they may have not yet had the opportunity to experience. The strains in blended family relationships will not fix themselves; to improve the quality of these relationships, someone must take initiative and must be persistent. I personally thrive off of peace. I've realized that when my family is at peace, things just fall in alignment. When there is a disturbance in our peace, that's when things are in disarray. Unless you want to spend a lifetime waiting for the dynamic of your blended family to change on its own as you watch the years pass you by, you will have to make the extra effort necessary to change the tone of your blended family relationships as necessary. If you want peace, be the peacekeeper.

II.

BLENDED FAMILY

PERSPECTIVES

One of the most powerful lessons that I've learned about blended family living is that it's critical to understand not only your own role as a stepparent, but to also understand the role and dynamics of everyone else involved. Once you understand everyone's position, you will be able to make more clear decisions on how to support your spouse and build harmony for your blended family.

Understanding Perspectives

The other parent's willingness to cooperate and peacefully interact with you will greatly depend upon the type of relationship that exists between them and your spouse. Of course if there has been a history of constant drama between them, they will likely be reluctant to welcome you. This is one of the reasons a lot of what's in this book is focused on your spouse and your support of them. You are often your spouse's greatest influence. The more you encourage and influence peace and cooperation through them, the greater the chance your entire blended family will reach the level of harmony you desire.

The first and most critical step to building harmony with the other parent is gaining an understanding of their perspective - what type of parent they are and the mental or emotional space they are in. By understanding, you can make informed decisions on how to invest in your blended family more effectively based on your circumstances.

While no parents are exactly the same, in blended families, I've noticed a common trend; there tend to be 5 different "categories" of parents: 1) The present parent, 2) The erratic parent; 3) The scorned parent, 4) The "Irrational" Parent; and 5) The deadbeat parent. What "category" your spouse and the other parent fall into will likely influence their perspective, tendencies, and in turn the best way to interact with them in an effort to create a harmonious blended family.

❖ *The Present Parent*

The present parent has a genuine interest in being the best parent possible regardless of what's happened or happening between them and the other parent. The present parent only has one role - that of being the other parent. The only thing they are concerned with at this point is what's best for their child. It doesn't matter how your spouse feels about them, how they feel about your spouse, or what happened in their relationship; that is no longer of concern to them. They are focused solely on raising their child at this moment and the only thing they are focused on is protecting the interests of their child and ensuring they have the best future possible.

If this is the other parent

If your stepchild's other parent is in this category, you and your spouse can consider yourselves to be in a better position than many blended families. Now, don't get me wrong, they are far from perfect. Just like you and your spouse, they make mistakes and bad decisions from time to time, but all in all, they are a good parent; they want your spouse to have a good relationship with their child, love them, have fun with them, teach them, guide them, support them, provide for them, and be involved in almost every aspect of their lives. They likely don't have an issue with the fact that your spouse has moved on. However, they will want to make sure that you have their child's best interest at heart and that you're in it for the long haul before they welcome you to the family. Once you break the initial barrier of reluctance, they will ultimately develop the same feelings about you as their child's stepparent and will appreciate your involvement and support for their child. So, if your child's other parent falls into this category, getting to a place of peace and cooperation when it comes to co-parenting won't be as challenging as you think. They have the potential to be the best parent to co-parent with; that is, if you fully understand and appreciate their role and position. A few tweaks in your and your spouse's mindset and approach in the way you handle your dealings and you'll be well on your way to the drama-free life you desire.

<u>If this is your spouse</u>

Hopefully your spouse falls into this category. If your spouse is no longer harboring any ill feelings toward the other parent, you won't have *as much* work from the inside. Your focus will be on getting both of you in the routine of operating with a business model mindset when working with the other parent. Making the leap into a business model mindset can drastically improve your situation, lessen the unnecessary drama, and hopefully encourage the other parent to make a conscious effort to do the same, no matter where they are right now. If not, at least you can rest assured knowing that you did your very best to try to establish a co-parenting partnership and you will also have the tools needed to remedy a lot of unnecessary problems and confusion, and to take whatever action is necessary to ensure that your spouse can be an active parent in their child's life.

❖ *The Erratic Parent*

Erratic parents are those unbalanced parents who love the *idea* of being a parent, but are inconsistent. Many parents complain that this parent "parents at their convenience." Although they enjoy the time they spend with their children, they often forget (or ignores) the fact that parenting is a full-time job, not just for one parent, but for both. They will take responsibility of their child if asked, but seldom take initiative. If they aren't in the mood to parent, they'll place the burden on the other parent without considering their schedule or feelings. They will spend time with their child, but come and go as they please. They make their own personal plans without considering who's going to take care of their child - assuming that the other parent will. If it's not "their turn" to care for their child, you better believe they are living young, wild, and free.

If this is the other parent

If this sounds like your stepchild's other parent, don't worry! The good news is, although erratic parents are inconsistent, with effort and guidance from you and your spouse as co-parents, it's likely they can make a smooth shift into that of a present parent. In most situations, the erratic parent isn't a *bad* parent. For whatever reason, he/she just doesn't quite understand or appreciate much of the dynamics of parenting, especially co-parenting. Erratic parents aren't that concerned about you being an active participant in their child's life. In fact, they likely appreciate all of the input and help that you provide in conjunction with your spouse, as that limits their responsibilities. Depending on how much parenting responsibility you are personally willing to assume, this could be a good or a frustrating thing. The key to having a positive, successful co-parenting relationship with the erratic parent is communication. Actually, communication is one of the key elements to all co-parenting relationships, but specifically to this one; you and/or your spouse clearly communicating about your expectations and limits is vital. You and/or your spouse may have to sit down and have a discussion about what you need from him or her to not only ensure that you're all on the same page but also to prevent their inconsistencies from being disruptive to your household.

If this is your spouse

Now, on the other hand, if your spouse fits the description of an erratic parent, it's important to support them in making a shift out of that category. When it comes to raising children in blended families, consistency is key. Lack of consistency can be detrimental to the well-being of your stepchild and it will also put a strain on your marriage. Consequently, your spouse has no room to be erratic; your stepchild must know that the two of you are reliable and that they can depend on you no matter what. You have to help your spouse figure out the type of relationship they want to have with their child. Do they just want to be the parent that does the minimum, dropping by as scheduled or as requested by the other parent, similar to that of a babysitter? Or do they want to be known as the co-parent who's fully active and involved in their child's life. It is my hope that they want the latter, because this is what their children need. They must not think of their parenting time with their child as "their time," and stop at that. They must make an effort to be involved in other aspects of their child's life that don't necessarily occur during scheduled parenting time. They must attend school events and meetings, participate in extracurricular activities, and take advantage of any additional time they have the opportunity to spend with their child. In other words, they must understand that they must go above and beyond for their child's benefit. If they aren't there yet, this is something you can facilitate by being a responsible investor in your blended family.

❖ *The Scorned Parent*

The scorned parent is probably one of the most confusing to deal with. Though they have a genuine interest in being a good parent to their child, *your spouse* on the other hand, is on their "s%$# list." If your spouse doesn't make a serious effort to nip the problems they have in the bud, your blended family situation will likely be extremely uncomfortable, as their attitude towards you and your spouse will remain unpredictable.

There are many reasons a parent can become scorned. Sometimes, it may be due to unresolved issues tied to their previous relationship with your spouse;

they've been lied to, cheated on, deceived, or otherwise disappointed and don't necessarily know how to handle the emotions that come with that territory. Sometimes, it may be due to the fact that the other parent still wants an intimate relationship with your spouse and they remain in a space of resentment caused by the circumstances surrounding or resulting in the end of their relationship.

The Space of resentment- You have to remember that regardless of how they feel now, at one point, your spouse and the other parent were a happy duo; either as a couple who was in love, dating to see if they were meant to be, or a fling who enjoyed each other for a season. Either way, at some point things were different between them. Then something happened and now things are the opposite. And to make matters worse, unlike when they first met, they now have a child together, so walking away and erasing each other from their lives is pretty much impossible. With that impossibility often comes residual hurt, pain, sadness, anger, and much more. Chances are, the other parent didn't want *"their* family" to separate to begin with. If deep down inside the other parent still desires to have an intimate relationship and family with your spouse, embracing the idea of having a blended family will be extremely challenging. When a relationship ends without a mutual understanding, commonly at least one person will be left trying to deal with the division and confusing emotions on their own while the other moves on without difficulty. Though you and/or your spouse's initial point of view may be "that's the other parent's problem, not ours!" This view could very well lead to problems for you.

Feeling unsupported through a time of family division can be an extremely uncomfortable situation that can very quickly escalate out of control. Hear me when I say this:

If you choose to disregard "their problem", your choice will have significant bearing on the type of co-parenting relationship you have with them; it may perhaps be the determining factor of whether your spouse will have "baby daddy/mama drama" or a cohesive co-parenting relationship.

The good news is, there are actions you can personally take in an effort to minimize this unnecessary drama. A lot of times, one thing we often overlook is another's need to be understood. We sometimes become so consumed in our own perception that we close our eyes to the needs of others. As people in general, one of the most frustrating things we experience in life is feeling like another does not appreciate, recognize, comprehend, or care about our feelings. While for one reason or another you may not actually "care" about the other parent's feelings, one thing is for certain, in blended families, a little empathy can go a long way and can even potentially influence change in the dynamic of your divided family, for the better. Just so we're clear, I'm not suggesting that you exhibit *sympathy* for the other parent. There's a pretty significant difference between sympathy and empathy. Sympathy is defined as *harmony of or agreement in feeling*. Suggesting that you have sympathy for the other parent would be unreasonable, as that would possibly insist upon you forcing feelings that don't exist. Empathy on the other hand, simply requires *the capacity to recognize emotions that are being experienced by another*. To take it even deeper, there are two types of empathy:

Affective Empathy - the ability to respond with an appropriate emotion to another's mental state, and

Cognitive Empathy - the ability to understand another's perspective or mental state.

To induce a positive co-parenting relationship, you and your spouse must demonstrate compassion for your co-parenting relationship, and the need to shift it into a more cooperative state. This requires you to be empathetic to the other parent's feelings. It may be surprising to know that accomplishing this is really not difficult at all; it simply entails you and your spouse recognizing the emotions that the other parent may be experiencing (specifically as it relates to their separation), making an effort to understand them, and responding with an appropriate emotion (an appropriate emotion being one of understanding rather than *not* caring).

A little empathy goes a long way.

Other times a parent may be scorned after things that have happened due to the nature of their tumultuous co-parenting relationship with your spouse, which has in essence left them in a space of frustration.

The Space of frustration- There are many reasons parents may be in the space of frustration, and chances are, if either parent is in this space, neither them nor your spouse is an innocent party. One (probably both) of them did (or didn't do) something that has contributed to this. It may just be because of the nature of the relationship between the parties, their inability to communicate peacefully with each other, constant disagreements, negative attitudes, inconsistent parenting habits, differing parenting styles, etc. They may, just be tired of it all. Parents in the frustrated space would rather just not bother. They often feel like things will just be easier if they do everything and make all decisions for their child on their own without interacting with the other parent. These parents operate as if they are a single parent, without regard to the other.

The problem with either parent being in this space is that although frustrations may be justified, the fact is that they are not single parents. There are two parents, both who have perspectives and input that matters. It's called co-parenting for a reason and the key to developing a co-parenting relationship with a parent in the frustrated space is recognizing the root of the frustration.

<u>If this is the other parent</u>

What part has your spouse played in all of this? The other parent likely didn't just wake up frustrated with your spouse one day. You may have to support your spouse through figuring out how they are contributing to the frustration and how they can address it with the other parent and start fresh in order to prevent them from recurring. For example, if the root of their frustration is due to your spouse's previous inconsistent parenting habits, you can help your spouse figure out a consistent parenting schedule that will work for all of you and propose the same to the other parent. If the frustrations are caused by inability to communicate peacefully, your spouse may want to consider communicating about sensitive subjects in writing; this would allow each parent to clearly express their thoughts without interruption and ponder each other's position before responding at the height of emotion. One of the most effective ways to get the other parent out of the frustrated space is to communicate and gain an understanding about their expectations and needs and make a commitment to put in greater effort going forward. This again goes back to having a little empathy. This process may require the assistance of a mediator (a trained neutral professional that works with parents to resolve these type of issues), but brainstorming solutions to these things can prove very beneficial. The good news is, if your spouse takes a positive step toward resolving the unsettled issues with them directly, they can transition into a cooperative co-parent. The bad news is, if these unsettled issues remain as-is, there's a great chance that they'll transition into "the irrational parent," which is the last thing your family needs.

The key to turning your co-parenting relationship with a scorned parent around goes back to the earlier discussion about dealing with the past and your attitude towards what you normally may consider to be "their problem." The solution is not to just ignore the issues as if they never occurred and don't matter. Just because you ignore your past, doesn't mean it goes away. The fact still remains that whatever happened between them and your spouse may still be hindering their ability to move forward. Remember, hurt people, hurt people. A great first step to remedying this situation is to help your spouse try to lessen the anger and frustration the other parent may be experiencing. The idea remains, a little empathy can go a long way.

<u>If this is your spouse</u>

If your spouse is the one scorned and in the space of frustration and ready to just throw in the towel when it comes to making an effort to co-parent, the first thing you must help them do to get out of this space is recognize accountability; what accountability have they (or even you) accepted for not being in a place of peace and cooperation with the other parent? Is it all the other parent's fault? Is it because the other parent is "difficult" or worse - "crazy" that they have not yet been able to co-parent without drama? More often than not, when speaking to divided/blended families about their situations, these are the sentiments expressed; the complaining parent often insists that the brunt of the problems that are being experienced lie solely in the other parent. When asked about their child's other parent, many parents cite that they just "deal with them" as necessary to maintain a relationship with their child. I get it. Sometimes due to the tumultuous relationship between the parents, it may seem like the easiest and best thing to do is to "deal" with the other parent as little as possible. But if this is the attitude you or your spouse currently have about the other parent and the route you choose to take, you are completely missing the notion of "co-parenting."

If you're currently in the space of frustration and have a mindset that you don't need to work with or involve the other parent regarding your children, your blended family harmony is essentially doomed from the start. While this state of mind will allow for little interaction between the parents, it's essential to shift out of that mindset, as it is of no benefit to the child, and that's what this is all about right?

Rather than looking at the other parent as someone you and your spouse have to "deal with," it's important to realize that if you want a life of peace and harmony, an effort on a level much higher than that of just "dealing" will be required. The effort you and your spouse put in will contribute to the type of relationship you both build or do not build with the child and the other parent. You both have a huge hand in whether your stepchild will grow up in a drama-filled situation or will instead grow up and experience a thriving relationship with all of you. You are now part of a blended family unit that must peacefully work together until your stepchild reaches 18 years old, and perhaps beyond. You have to *build* the life you want. Your spouse will need your support to see and build the bigger picture - to stop "dealing" and start building.

The only way to do this, is for your spouse to learn how to "get over it," whatever "it" is that makes them have the ill feelings they have toward their child's other parent. Whether these feelings consist of frustration, anger, hate, or distrust, they have to find a way to get over that and adopt the business model mindset previously discussed so they can focus on what's most important - building harmony in this now blended family so you can live in peace and so that the children involved can thrive. That's where you come in! As the only one in this blended family with an objective perspective, you can support your spouse by helping them reach their full co-parenting potential with the other parent, thereby creating a peaceful zone for your family.

❖ *The Irrational Parent*

(A.K.A. "The Crazy Baby Daddy/Mama")

Irrational, selfish, not concerned about the welfare or best interests of their child, unreasonable, with an agenda centered on vengeance and making your spouse's life miserable. Sound familiar? This is the irrational parent (also known as "The Crazy Baby Daddy/Mama"). When I'm contacted by parents and even stepparents who are seeking help for their spouses to resolve issues related to their divided/blended family, the most commonly cited problem is a "crazy baby daddy/mama."

Although oftentimes people nonchalantly refer to the other parent as "crazy," more often than not, there is nothing crazy about them at all. When asked why they are "crazy," answers given usually describe a scorned parent or a present parent that doesn't deal with nonsense. A parent does not automatically qualify as "crazy" simply because they disagree with the other parent (in this case your spouse), left them, has ill feelings towards them, doesn't get along with them, or *justifiably* (←**key word**) won't allow them to see their child. After all, certain circumstances create logical reason for all of these things. As far as I'm concerned, every parent that's being labeled as a "crazy baby daddy/mama" will initially get the benefit of the doubt. But, there are certain actions that would make one undeserving of that benefit, and may reasonably justify a belief that the parent is in fact a "crazy baby daddy/mama."

Now, before I get too deep into this, let me first disclaim that I <u>personally</u> despise the use of the terms "baby daddy" and "baby mama" in real life. So, when you see it used herein, understand, that I am not encouraging use of the term to refer to either parent; the use within this book is solely for illustrative and quotation purposes.

Almost everyone knows at least one "irrational parent;" whether they are in fact your stepchild's other parent, a relative, close friend, someone you are acquainted with, or even your spouse. They are the parent that refuses to let go of the past and consciously puts their own emotions before the best interest of their child. Suffering from emotional instability, they oftentimes make decisions based on their emotions at a particular moment, without regard to how it will affect their child's future. Consequently, in some instances they will alienate the child from the other parent, abuse the child, neglect the child, and sometimes worse just to "get back at" the other parent. This makes them not only the most frustrating and complicated parent to deal with, but in some cases, also the most dangerous. The key to dealing with an irrational parent is tactful action; the way you and your spouse approach every situation will likely have great influence on the outcome of that situation.

Fighting Fires - The key to handling an irrational parent

Have you ever heard the saying, "you can't fight fire with fire"? Well, that phrase isn't to be interpreted literally. After all, in actuality you can fight fire with fire; it's done by professionals all the time. Once, while watching the news there was a huge story about an out of control fire that spread throughout one of the major Canyons in Southern California. The fire was spreading so rapidly due to high wind speeds that the standard methods normally used to put out fires were unsuccessful. So, specialists decided to use more advanced methods, including what they refer to as "back burning," a method of controlled burning. The idea of "back burning" is that by intentionally starting small fires along the main fire front, the small fires will burn back towards the large fire that is out of control and in essence, little flammable material will exist by the time the fire reaches the burnt area.

So what's the point? You can't successfully fight fire without specific skill and *intention*. It would never be wise to just go recklessly starting fires simply because another fire is out of control and expect to resolve the problem. The key to fighting a fire with fire is that in order to do so successfully, you must be a "professional," a "specialist." You must be tactful. This same principle should be applied in real life encounters with others, especially your stepchild's other parent. If you don't like the way things are going, change what you can. The analogy to fire-fighting and co-parenting as an "investor" in your blended family is that, as a professional, reasonable parent and stepparent, there will be times when changing your strategy is necessary in order to put out the fire you and your spouse are dealing with.

For example, there was one man whose ex-wife was so distraught that the marriage ended, she became extremely irrational. She did everything within her power on a quest for vengeance to make his life miserable; everything from alienating their child from him, using the child as a pawn, obtaining a restraining order against him by making false allegations of threats made against her, defaming him, and even stalking him. Understandably, his first inclination in reaction to her behavior was outrage. Instead, he took the approach of a professional parent; he sought legal counsel, had the false charges dropped, established official orders for child custody, and secured a restraining order against her as well as an order that she seek counseling and anger management classes. Although he didn't stoop to her level and respond in an irrational manner, he also did not sit idly by and endure her behavior without taking any action at all. In my uncontrollable fire example above, when the city couldn't stop the fire from spreading, they changed their approach; they brought in a professional whose specialty is "back burning." Similarly, when this husband's situation got out of hand, he fought fire with fire by acting as a professional co-parent, tactfully taking control of his situation.

You and your spouse must learn to be and think of yourself as professional parents, whose specialty is The Business of Co-Parenting for the best interest of your stepchild, even in difficult situations. While you can't change your stepchild's other parent's behavior or the fact that they are your stepchild's other parent, you and your spouse can shift *your* mindsets. Be the "back burner": Think about what YOU two can do differently to influence change. If someone you are dealing with is combative and always wants to argue and fight, don't take part in it. Refuse to participate in any quarrels and let the person know how to reach you when they are done arguing with themselves. If you want to be respected, show respect. If you want consideration, show some consideration. And remember that change happens for others when THEY are ready. It's not going to happen overnight. But if you constantly greet someone who's combative with a generous smile (no matter how much you'd rather just fire back on them), eventually they won't have a choice but to smile back. Any other responsive behavior would simply make them appear psychotic for continuing to argue with themselves.

With this in mind, although you can't change your stepchild's other parent's behavior, you must take the appropriate, tactful steps that will influence them to change themself. If they need counseling or some other type of professional help, you and your spouse must figure out the best way to ensure that either 1) they get the help they need or 2) their failure to get this help does not detrimentally affect the best interests or well-being of your stepchild. The hardest part about dealing with the irrational parent is figuring out the most practical approach you should take in order to accomplish this task. Because there is obvious tension in your relationship with them, they are not likely to accept advice or suggestions about their coping needs from you or your spouse. Perhaps you can seek the assistance of someone who is close to them to help them understand that counseling or some other type of intervention would be beneficial for them in dealing with the dynamics of the blended family.

As you can see, there are many different directions a blended family relationship with an irrational parent can take. Your goal is to support your spouse in finding and taking the most practical roads that will ultimately lead to safety and peace. Depending on the severity of their irrationality and your circumstances, this may require seeking help from a lawyer, the Department of Children and Family Services/Child Protective Services, and/or the court system. Consequently, the success of your personal efforts and said interventions will influence whether they will transition from irrational to the present parent, or will diminish to a deadbeat.

❖ *The Deadbeat Parent*

It is my hope that neither your spouse nor your stepchild's other parent's actions are in alignment with America's most prevalent and least favorite topic - the deadbeat parent. First, let me say, in my opinion, the term "deadbeat" is overused and misused. Whenever I hear someone call a parent a deadbeat, I usually ask: "What makes them a deadbeat?" The overwhelming response is always some variation of "because they don't have any money or pay child support." Huh? Is that it? Because they can't or don't pay money, that makes them a deadbeat? Confused by this, I decided to look up the term deadbeat to get a better understanding of the term. To my surprise, definitions I found were almost identical to the common responses I received. Most legal definitions of a "deadbeat" included references of a "parent who fails to pay child support."

Let me be clear, I understand that finances are important however, considering the fact that being a parent requires much more important characteristics than "having money," I find this to be an absurd definition that is completely unfair because the definition is extremely broad and insensitive of specific circumstances. There are so many different circumstances that can lead to one's failure to pay child support. Specifically, and most commonly, Stuff Happens! Life is not perfect. Sometimes a parent may genuinely, temporarily be unable to afford to make substantial financial contributions to their child's life. With the way the economy fluctuates, even those with higher education and a lot of work experience have found themselves unemployed, underemployed, or otherwise struggling to make ends meet. Does this mean that parent should be labeled a "deadbeat" or not able to see their child because of their financial situation? Absolutely not! If that were the case, there would be a ridiculous increase in the amount of children who are parentless because financial problems affect both mothers and fathers. Automatically deeming one who does not pay child support (irrespective of specific circumstances, including any other contributions made to their child's life) a deadbeat is shallow and ridiculous.

Let's look at it another way, what about the parents who do contribute financially, but that is all they do? Is that enough? People tend to forget that it takes much more than money to raise a child. One can pay all the money in the world in child support and still be a deadbeat. Society has us so wrapped up in riches and material things that we often disregard what is more important. Yes, it does take money to raise a child: children need food, clothing, shelter, and other necessaries of life. However, a child who has the necessaries of life, but does not have the time, attention, love and support they need from their parents is a lost child. Even if a parent is unable to provide financially, they should be able to contribute to their child's life in other aspects without being labeled as a deadbeat. There are plenty of parents who may be struggling financially, yet are phenomenal parents.

I believe that we should all re-define the word "deadbeat." My definition of a "deadbeat" is:

One who deliberately fails to provide financial support for their child and/or refuses or fails to make reasonable efforts to be involved in their child's life as a parent.

Stepping Out of the Deadbeat Zone

If this is the other parent

So here's the thing: People make dumb decisions and mistakes sometimes. And **choosing** to be a deadbeat or otherwise absent from your child's life is considered to be one of them. The good news is that sometimes, people change. Sometimes, later on in life after years have been missed from their child's life, a "deadbeat" parent may finally decide to make an effort to change. They may contact your spouse and acknowledging their mistakes, their absence, and try to make things right with their child. Although later than ideal, this *could be* good for your stepchild, as they may have longed for a relationship with that absent parent.

This may be extremely hard for your spouse to fathom or even for you to fathom if you've stepped into the place of that absent parent and took on what would have and should have been their responsibilities. And while your feelings are absolutely justifiable, the uncomfortable reality is that in many states, unless there is a *legally* established reason that parent shouldn't have any type of relationship with your stepchild (the child has been adopted or other legal orders have been made that terminate their right to custody or visitation), their rights remain and they can seek court assistance to enforce these rights. So, rather than being completely dismissive to the idea of reunification, when faced with a situation like this, understand, that if done right, their reunification with your stepchild may be successful and there are stipulations that can be put in place to ensure your stepchild's protection (see below).

<u>If this is your spouse</u>

That said, if your spouse is the one who is or has been in the "deadbeat" zone, hopefully you can help them change that. In my experience, I've met and worked with distressed parents, most of them fathers, but also a few mothers, who were not actively involved in their child's lives nearly as much as they wanted to be. While reasons for their absence varied, many of them complained that it was impossible to be involved because they constantly had to deal with drama from the other parent. Others admitted to being absent because at the time their child was born, they were "not ready" for a child. Some claimed their absence was not their choice, but that they were denied the opportunity to establish and maintain a relationship with their child by their child's other parent. Regardless of the reason, a parent's absence from their child's life can be detrimental to that child.

Absent parents are often automatically put into the "deadbeat" zone, whether they deserve to be there or not. The bad news is once you're in the deadbeat zone, getting out will be a journey full of twists and turns, to say the least. The good news is there *is* a way out.

If your spouse has found themself in the deadbeat zone, don't fret. With your support and their commitment to doing so, it's possible to get out of that zone, but it requires: **P**ersistence, **U**rgency, **S**elflessness, and **H**ealing.

Persistence is key because you may not achieve the results you seek the first go-round, the second, or even the third. Factors such as the reason your spouse has been absent, the length of their absence, the relationship that is or is not already established with their child, the child's wishes, etc. are all things that will likely influence the transition out of the deadbeat zone. For example, if their absence is the result of alienation caused by their child's other parent, they may get out of the deadbeat zone sooner than if they purposefully chose to abandon their child due to the happenings of their life at that particular time. Not to say that the latter would make it impossible for your spouse to build/re-build a relationship with their child, but it may take longer.

This is where *Urgency* comes in. The only way that they will push through the deadbeat zone is if doing so is important to them. Developing a better relationship with their child can no longer only be something they simply think about or want. It must become a necessity. If not, the first opposition they face will cause them to become discouraged or throw in the towel. They will likely be up for a battle. It's up to them to prepare for that battle. What are they willing to do and/or endure so they can win, for their child? It will be far from a walk in the park.

For this reason, it's imperative that you help your

spouse understand and take on the characteristic of _Selflessness_. The bad news is, if they are in the deadbeat zone, chances are, they have not yet learned the art of selflessness. Selflessness would not allow one to abandon their child because they "weren't ready" to be a parent or "can't deal" with the child's other parent. Selflessness wouldn't allow one to concede to the other parent's interference with their relationship with their child. If they don't have a relationship with their child, the lack of a relationship ultimately lies on them because even if their child's other parent refuses to "allow" them to see their child, there are definitely remedies available to resolve that problem. Selflessness is defined as _putting someone else's needs, interests, or wishing before your own_. In essence, selflessness will require you to make a lot of sacrifices. I suggest that you help your spouse become more assertive and insist – in a positive way – that they are provided with more time with their child as well as counseling with their child if necessary. Show the child's other parent that they are dependable and reliable and that you will be supporting them in their parenting. Help them begin with baby steps in developing or re-developing a relationship with their child. Encourage them to visit with their child as much as possible and request an increase in the time appropriately.

This will not be an easy breezy process, especially in the beginning. You will have a lot of moments where you and/or your spouse may experience discomfort, frustration, anger, sadness, happiness, anxiety, and more. The key here is to remind them of why you are going through this battle together. Help them remember that it's not necessarily about them, it's about their child. Their child is depending on them to push through the deadbeat zone and into the equal parenting zone so that they may enjoy their presence in their life. Your spouse's ability to learn selflessness will be one of the factors that determines whether their child will become a statistic as mentioned above or the opposite.

The last, yet most important thing to keep in mind is that this process requires _Healing_. Healing for each party involved: your spouse, your stepchild, and their other parent. One thing that many parents who struggle to push through the deadbeat zone fail to realize is that this healing takes time, effort, and for you in particular, it will take a lot of endurance which is one of the most important characteristics you must have when making this transition. After all, if your spouse has been absent from their child's life, their perception of your spouse is likely not very optimistic. If your spouse _chose_ to miss out on their life, it's to be expected that their child and the other parent will both carry many ill feelings that will take time to heal. Additionally, they both, along with any other loved ones, will lack trust in your spouse. Trust is something that must be earned, especially if it's lost due to your spouse's own actions. In order to gain trust, your spouse must demonstrate their worthiness of it through their actions; show and prove.

Unfortunately, the same is true even in circumstances where your stepchild was alienated from your spouse against their will, because it's probable that your stepchild's perception was tainted by the other parent. Whatever the case may be, it's important that you and your spouse understand that your stepchild is in a vulnerable state, and is likely experiencing confusion, hurt, and many other feelings. So, while you both may be hurt by what has transpired, you must remember your stepchild's feelings of hurt that are just as valid, and work hard to get to a position where you can make things right for him or her. The only way to accomplish this is by supporting your spouse as they push through the deadbeat zone, because once they're out, they will be able to develop a relationship with their child like never before. They'll be able to teach him or her many things they need in order to thrive and be successful in life. Some of those lessons will come from your spouse's personal mistakes, others will simply come from wisdom. Either way, these will be things only your spouse will be able to give your stepchild, and your family's life will hopefully change for the better.

Regardless of whether the other parent or your spouse is attempting to get out of the deadbeat zone, here are a few things to consider when attempting to establish or re-establish a relationship for your stepchild after a parent's extensive absence or alienation:

Reunification counseling – If your stepchild's other parent has been absent for a significant period of time and had no contact or very minimal contact with your stepchild, there will likely be a lot of emotional issues that need to be addressed for the reunification to be successful. Qualified Marriage and family therapists and other counselors offer counseling and other support services that lesson or otherwise resolve the upset and uncertainty that comes with the territory of having an absent parent.

Supervised visits- Both you, your spouse, and your stepchild may be uncomfortable with your stepchild visiting with their other parent alone after long stretches of absence. When this is the case, supervised visits (requiring the presence of either a professional monitor, counselor, or trusted family member during visitation) will put your family at ease, while also allowing quality time with their other parent. This is a good way to start.

Step-up visitation plan- When children haven't seen their other parent for a long time, they may hit it off right after commencing or resuming their contact, or it may take a while. Until you see how things go, it's good to start things off slow to avoid unnecessary overwhelm. A step-up plan is essentially a visitation plan that builds up as time goes on. For example, you may start with 3 supervised visits and then graduate to 1 unsupervised day visit, and then multiple unsupervised daytime visits, and eventually progress to an overnight visit, and hopefully routine overnight weekends. How long each phase takes will really depend on your stepchild and how he or she adjusts to their other parent; it could take weeks, months, or years. It's a good idea to put a plan in place, test it to see how things go, and adjust accordingly.

III.

BLENDED FAMILY TRANSITIONS

Blending a family is definitely a process. There are a lot of new adjustments that everyone in your family must make. It's important to be mindful of everyone's feelings in the process of getting used to all of the new dynamics of your family in order to build harmony within.

Figuring out where you stand with the other parent may very well be one of the most awkward things you may face as a stepparent. Out of all of the new things a divided family must adjust to, most parents report the most difficult being the adjustment to new people in their child's life, specifically the other parent's new significant other - YOU. Don't take it personal; this has absolutely nothing to do with you. Where you stand will depend on many different things including your spouse's relationship with the other parent, the other parent's attitude, and how you entered the family.

Remember, everyone in a blended family is coming from a place of loss. And while it would be lovely to be welcomed by everyone with open arms, in most cases that would be unrealistic. Firstly, it's natural for a parent to have some reservations about new people coming into their child's life. After all, this is *their child* we are talking about here and it's their duty as his or her mother or father to look out for their best interest. Considering the fact that you are the equivalent of a stranger, reluctance is not unreasonable. I get it. I have three children and just the thought of the wrong person entering into their lives makes me very uncomfortable. Besides, in this world we're living in, some people are crazy! You may not be, but some people are. I'm sure you've seen some of the news headlines where situations with the new significant other and the children just went all bad. No one wants this for their child, so as a precaution, you may get the side-eye at first, just understand where they may be coming from and don't immediately take it personal, because chances are - it's not.

Secondly, you must remember that you are walking into a pre-existing situation. You don't know every single thing that's transpired between your spouse, their child, and the other parent. So, depending on the history of this family before you joined, quite frankly, everyone just may not be ready for the addition of a new person. Again, this likely has nothing to do with you. Because everyone in a blended family is coming from a place of loss, it may just not be possible for them to see the gain and benefit of your presence just yet, and that's okay.

The power of the unknown

You may be surprised to know that ironically, the same uncertainty you feel about your stepchild's other parent's perception of you is the same uncertainty they have about your perception of them. Think about it: You married your spouse, which essentially means that you are your spouse's biggest supporter. Your spouse is *their* ex. Now you know that when you are in a relationship with someone, especially a marriage, you typically share EVERYTHING with that person- the good, the bad, and the ugly. So, considering the fact that the other parent knows that your spouse has shared the good, the bad, and the ugly about their relationship, their problems, and their previous drama, and that there's a chance that your spouse has portrayed them in a negative light, it's understandable for them to be uncertain about your preconceived notions about them. So, while you may come into the blended family with the intention of remaining objective, *they don't know that.* Though you may come into the blended family with the intention of building harmony for the best interest of everyone involved, they don't know that either. They don't know the type of person that you are. They don't know that you have their child's best interest at heart. They don't know if you're around for the long haul or if you're just another passerby. They don't know if you will treat their child like your own or if you'll treat them like a stepchild (you know...like the stepmother in Cinderella). They don't know if you are full of drama. They don't know if you will just blindly support your spouse regardless of whether they're right or wrong. Their perspective of you is completely based on the unknown. For this reason, it's important that you make the unknown, known. And it all starts with your introduction.

Your official introduction

In all blended families, an official introduction (or at least an offer of a formal introduction) is necessary in order to foster harmony. Having the opportunity to be formally introduced to the other parent facilitates the greatest potential for a positive relationship with them. This is true regardless of whether you are newly married or have been married for a while. In my opinion, it's never too late for an introduction. If you're newly married, an introduction can set the tone of your blended family relationship. If you've been married for a while, but the dynamics have been strained, a formal introduction can re-set the tone of your blended family.

To facilitate this, your spouse should let the other parent know that they're interested in strengthening the dynamic of the family and offer a sit-down with you and the other parent (and their spouse if they're re-married) to discuss how you can all collaborate for the best interest of their child going forward. They may say yes or they may decline, but by putting the ball in their court and giving them the option, they will see both that you and your spouse are consciously making an effort to co-parent with them and keep them informed and involved in major decisions that will essentially affect your child. They may not like the fact that your spouse is moving on, but at least she or he can't say that you didn't make an effort to work with them. I know this seems like a lot, but it's a very important part of the business of co-parenting.

Even if the other parent did not show your spouse this same courtesy I am suggesting, remember to always lead by example. Show them the right way to co-parent and hopefully they will eventually follow. One of the key characteristics of a good co-parent is the ability to be the bigger person no matter what the other parent does. Do not expect them to lead your blended family in the direction that it should go, as that may be unrealistic at this time. You may have to step up and be proactive! You want to neutralize as many potentially negative situations as possible. By attempting to facilitate a formal meeting with you and the other parent, you and your spouse are making a deliberate effort to shift things to a more positive and cooperative note. This is much better than just getting married without acknowledging the fact that this is a transition for your family that will require collaboration for it to be successful. This also reassures the other parent that you are not trying to replace their role in their child's life and may even encourage them to take the lead in getting to know you and to incorporate you into their blended family.

If you have the opportunity for a formal introduction, make the most of it. This is the time to recognize your role in your stepchild's life and acknowledge that you understand the boundaries. This is the time to have a candid conversation with the other parent and let them know that you have their child's best interest at heart and will always do what's best for them and encourage your spouse to do the same. This is the time that you assure them that you understand the importance of your role as a stepparent and that you understand that your presence will have a substantial impact on their child, the type of life they have, and the person they become, and reassure them that you will do your best to be a great example for them. Let them know that you are there to support their child, them, and your spouse as much as possible and that you're on their (your blended family's) team.

If the other parent declines a formal introduction, don't worry. They probably just have to get accustomed to the idea of you being around, but it will more than likely happen eventually. Even if you are in a situation where the other parent is full of drama, refuses to build a relationship with you, but would rather fight and overall just create a negative situation, getting to a place of harmony is not impossible, it will just take time. It all goes back to the foundation - maintaining a business model mindset. You must consistently lead by example and tactfully fight fires as necessary and remain the professional parent regardless of how irrational the other parent chooses to act. Remember, people cannot keep up drama with themselves, if they can that's when it's likely that they are crazy and need to seek professional help. The more reasonable you are, the more reasonable she or he will likely and eventually become. Although it may seem like *eventually* will never come, at some point, something has to give. Just continue to do the right thing, put your stepchild's best interest first, and things will fall into place.

If you were to see our blended family today, you'd think that we've been a happy blended family forever. We attend sporting and school events, parties, parent-teacher conferences, and anything else that comes up together. And if one of us can't make it, we report what happened to the other so they're always in the loop. Although it now feels like magic, we didn't get here magically. It took persistence, dedication, and work. My stepson's mother and I met several times before mutually acknowledging that we were on the same team. Although I'd always wanted to develop a good relationship with her for our son, it took us quite a while to get there. I thought she hated me. The reality is, she didn't hate me per se, she just didn't know me. She didn't know what kind of person I was, how long I'd be around, and my intentions. Though we saw each other regularly (almost weekly), our interaction was minimal. There were times that we'd literally be sitting within a few feet of each other and didn't acknowledge each other's presence...no "hello", no "how are you?" - nothing. Believe it or not, we didn't have our "formal" introduction until years of my husband and I being together. Although we'd had several brief conversations in passing, it wasn't until we needed each other for our son that we established each other as "teammates" rather than adversaries. It wasn't until we realized that if we all didn't get on the same page, that our son would be headed in the direction of the negative statistics I referenced at the beginning of this book. The bottom line is, being a part of a blended family is not easy, especially for the parents. In fact, it's one of the most complicated things that you will have to do because there are so many different people involved, with so many different personalities, mindsets, and points of view. Again, the business of co-parenting is not something that comes naturally; it is a skill, a much defined one that requires constant conscious effort and will hopefully develop into a lifestyle.

Blended Family Coaching

If you find that you and your spouse are having a difficult time transitioning into a blended family and co-parenting with the other parent due to high conflict or non-cooperation on their part, incorporating the strategies in self-help books such as this one may suffice. However, if you need a little more hands-on guidance or help incorporating the principles in this book into your life, you may want to consider a live co-parenting course or a life coach.

There are many different types of co-parenting courses offered throughout the country. In many high conflict cases, some judges will require parents to complete these courses as part of a court order. Some courses are available for the parents to attend individually, while others require the parents to attend together. Courses are often short term (usually no more than a few weeks) and may be conducted in either a small or large group setting and allow parents to openly discuss and learn solutions to issues that are common amongst divided/blended families.

A life coach is a professional who helps clients set and achieve personal goals. A co-parent coach is a life coach whose job is to help you identify and take tactful action toward goals for your divided/blended family. A coach will work with you and your spouse individually or even in conjunction with the other parent, by getting to know you, helping enhance the things that you are doing well, and adjust the areas that are not working or which can be done better. In a sense, a co-parent/blended family coach can serve as a facilitator in helping you accomplish your full parenting potential despite your differences and difficulties with the other parent. Unlike counseling, the emphasis of coaching is not placed on what has happened in the past; coaching is geared towards your present circumstances, thoughts and actions and how to shift them in order to positively impact your future. Because your coach will fully understand your concerns and ultimate goals, he or she will refer you to other resources or professionals, such as a counselor, if necessary.

New schedule

An important aspect of blended family living is establishing a schedule that will allow your stepchildren to spend time with both households - you and your spouse's home as well as their other parent's. It is an established fact that it's in a child's best interest that he or she has frequent and continuing contact with both parents (absent extreme circumstances of course). Although your spouse may be accustomed to taking things day by day, without any structured schedule, unless your spouse and your child's other parent have a very good relationship and understanding, co-parenting day by day is *not* a good idea. Just as your family has a work schedule, school schedule, sports schedule, and extra-curricular activity schedule, it's important that you also establish a *parenting schedule* and then make adjustments to it day to day as necessary. Hopefully, your spouse, and the other parent can do this between themselves rather than having a family court decide. This may be hard to accomplish at first, but it is possible and can make all the difference in whether you will have a successful co-parenting experience or a grueling one.

To start, you will need to consider all of your schedules and your stepchild's schedule (including school, tutoring, sports, extra-curricular activities, church, etc.) and determine which household will be responsible for your child on which dates and times. You will need to consider holidays, birthdays, spring and summer breaks, vacations, etc. You should also discuss other things that are of importance to you such as communication with the child while he or she is with the other parent, what happens if one of you are unable to have the child on your agreed upon day, where your custody exchanges will take place, what happens if a parent is late, your method of communication (i.e., email, text message, phone calls, a co-parent journal, etc.)

As the new member of this family, you may want to be as actively involved in your stepchild's life as your spouse and the other parent, and it is my hope that at some point you will be. However, until you establish this type of co-parenting relationship, you and your spouse will have to confer about things related to your blended family amongst yourselves. Behind the scenes, you can help your spouse make decisions about a practical schedule for your household and how you'll be able to assist them in parenting when your child is at your home by discussing these things with your spouse directly. Your spouse can then relay his or her proposals or requests to the other parent on their own.

New Home Life

The transition into a new blended family is exactly that - a transition - and in order to make the process as smooth as possible, it is important that your spouse maintain as much consistency as possible for the sake of their child. If you and your spouse move to a new home, try not to change your stepchild's school districts/schools unless absolutely necessary. It's important to maintain as many of the same routines that were in place prior to blending your family. The key here is not to *avoid* change, but to minimize additional and unnecessary change until your stepchild has adjusted to this new, blended family situation.

Parents excited about their new marriage and blending their family often overlook how this affects their children. While family is obviously important to a child, so is his or her familiar social life. Making sudden moves in the midst of what may already be a difficult transition can potentially be traumatizing for your stepchild. You and your spouse will have to consider more than just your own feelings and think about how this will affect your stepchild. While some children adjust quickly without issue, others must be guided through this process delicately.

Your Stepchild's Adjustment

You definitely don't get a manual on stepparenting when you marry someone with children. Consequently, when stepping into a blended family, it's hard to know what to really expect. Because all children are different and have been through different circumstances, the best advice I can give you is to expect the unexpected, but don't expect a miracle. Stepparenting is a journey to say the least. I remember when I was younger. My mom was a single mom. When she started dating my stepdad, I was ecstatic. He made her extremely happy, and was really nice to me. I loved the idea of him being around...until he proposed to my mom. At that moment it felt like a ton of bricks had just hit me. I was devastated. He couldn't marry my mom! If he married my mom, it would no longer be just me and her. I mean, dating her was cool, but marrying her!? I was not trying to hear that. From that point on, I gave him the hardest time. Though I didn't lose my home training and resort to disrespect, I shut him out. I cried, I pouted, and I complained, all for no justifiable reason at all, other than the idea that if he married my mom, I may lose something. Nothing in particular, just something. In hindsight, it was the most ridiculous reaction ever. He was and still is the greatest stepparent one could ever ask for. He stepped right into a parental role for me and treated me like his own. He's supported me through every experience in my life and walked me down the aisle when I got married. He's been great from the start, yet I cried.

This is the perfect example of the rollercoaster of emotions your stepchild may experience when you join their family. One moment they may be happy, one they may be sad. One moment they may be excited that you're joining their family, the next they may feel like you're taking something away from their family. One minute they'll crown you the stepparent of the year, the next they'll consider you the wicked stepparent similar to the one in Cinderella. Don't worry, I think this is all just part of the territory of blending a family. Just like you don't know what to expect, neither do they. So whatever you do, don't expect a miracle.

Rather, expect uncertainty from both of you. It's likely that there will not be an immediate attachment from either of you. And it could take forever to feel like you have a parent-child like bond. Understand that just like the other parent, they are likely coming from a place of loss. They have either lost their other parent through death, divorce, or their parents otherwise deciding not to continue their intimate relationship. If they had the opportunity to witness their parents together intimately, their separation could be devastating to them. Consequently, just as the other parent may not have welcomed you with arms stretched wide, your stepchild may not either. Again, this likely has nothing to do with you personally. So, don't take it personal.

❖ *Let Your Stepchild Set the Tone*

One mistake stepparents make when transitioning into a blended family is expecting instant love. It may be a while before you and your stepchild get to a place of love and gratification for each other. Depending on your stepchild's perspective, they may develop this love for you almost instantly, or they may be reluctant to let you in. The key here is to be patient and give them some time to get used to you being in their life and to set the tone. Don't try to rush it. Love takes time. Make sure you spend an adequate amount of time with your stepchild, both one-on-one and with your spouse and other children. Learn about the things they love to do and make arrangements for them to do it. Get to know more about what they struggle with and support them in that regard.

❖ *Have Empathy*

As mentioned previously: A little empathy goes a long way. It's important that you make an effort to connect with your stepchild and learn more about their perspectives. They may be uncomfortable with their parent marrying you. They may be uneasy about the new transitions that come with that territory. They may be experiencing anxiety due to the way the other parent makes them feel about you or your spouse. They may have been taught by the other parent to be disrespectful to you or to otherwise resist connecting with you. Just understand that this whole process will take them some time to get used to and sort through.

❖ *Love as Your Own*

Understand that it's absolutely okay to love your stepchild as your own child. Never let anyone, including the other parent, make you feel guilty for loving your stepchild, supporting them, doing for them, and caring for them just as you would if they were your biological child. I believe one of the reasons children in blended families experience more conflict in the home and need psychological counseling at higher rates is due to the disconnect they often feel once their family is blended. When you willingly spread your love to your stepchildren, they may feel less of a need to compete with you and your children for attention, affection, or connection, and may feel more of a sense of normalcy in your family. It only makes sense; if you want everyone to function like a family, you have to create a sense of belonging and a strong family aura.

If you have biological children of your own, you have to be very conscious about both their and your stepchild's feelings. If you support your children's extracurricular activities, make sure you do the same for your stepchild. If you purchase gifts for your biological children, make sure you do that for your stepchild as well. Your stepchildren should have the same benefits and responsibilities as your biological children. Though you may want to let your spouse take responsibility for enforcing discipline policies in your home, if your children are disciplined for breaking certain rules, make sure that same set of rules applies to your stepchildren. If your children are rewarded for certain activities or behavior, make sure those same benefits apply for your stepchildren. Eliminating division as much as possible will foster a closer bond with your stepchildren. It will help them understand that your love is not conditional, that you care about their well-being and their future, and that your love has no limits distinguished by DNA.

❖ *Set Boundaries*

All relationships require healthy boundaries. This is no different for your relationship with your stepchild. One of the first boundaries you will need to set is that of respect. Your stepchild's level of respect for you at the outset will likely depend on their relationship with your spouse, the other parent, and their attitude about your entry into their now blended family.

Be prepared for the "you're not my mom/dad" or "you can't tell me what to do" phase and nip that issue in the bud at the outset. Make sure your stepchild understands that you're not trying to replace their parent, but are simply joining their mom and dad in taking care of them. Establish that although you're not the other parent, you have their best interest at heart and expect them to follow the rules set while they are with you.

As mentioned above, establishing/maintaining a level of stability is a vital factor that will influence the dynamic of your relationship with your stepchild. Try to not only maintain the traditions that have already been established previously, but also to set new traditions with your blended family that are independent of their typical daily routine.

IV.

BLENDED

FAMILY LAW

In order to protect your blended family from unnecessary interruptions and prevent unnecessary problems, the most important thing you and your spouse need to understand are your legal rights and obligations.

Your spouse's legal rights

One of the most common questions I'm typically asked by stepparents is "what are my spouse's legal rights?"

An important thing you must understand is that unless there is a legally established reason that a parent should not have rights to their children, typically, in most states both parents have parental rights. The key is taking the initiative to legally *establish* these rights. One of the most common complaints I hear from parents in divided families is that the other parent interferes with their relationship with their child; the other parent:

- *"won't allow me to see my child."*
- *"doesn't answer the phone when I call to speak with my child."*
- *"always makes a scene and wants to argue."*
- *"lies and spreads rumors about me."*
- *"talks bad about me in front of my child."*
- *"makes my child say bad things about me."*

Trust me, I've heard and even seen it all. My question to any parent who makes these complaints is always: "What have you done to resolve these problems?" Sadly, most admit to taking little or no action. This was commonly either due to feeling as though they had no recourse or simply because it was easier to ignore the problem without challenge.

One of the most beneficial things your spouse can do for your blended family is establish child custody and/or visitation orders. Formal custody orders make divided/blended family life a little less complicated. Not only will it create a legal record as to who has the authority to make decisions related to your stepchild, but it will also outline who your stepchild will live with, what the other parent's visitation will be (if any), and much more. It can even include provisions such as phone time and orders that neither parent shall make disparaging remarks about the other in the presence or hearing distance of the minor children. If these orders are put into place, when a parent violates the orders, they could be at risk of monetary sanctions, a change in custody, or worse - jail time.

Many families make the mistake of skipping this step because they don't realize the consequences of not having enforceable orders. It's important to know that despite what you and your spouse may believe is the best custody/visitation arrangement for your stepchildren, unless your spouse and the other parent agree on these arrangements, custody is not automatic. While it is true that often mothers are granted custody, if a father wants custody, he can be granted custody as well. I see it happen every day, I help fathers do this every day, so never assume that "dad", can't have custody.

Here's why I'm telling you all of this. I want you to help your spouse understand that regardless of what the other parent may say or do, they have a place in their child's life just as much as the other parent does. Depending on the circumstances, they may have to put in a little extra work or effort to establish that place, but it's still their place…if they want it that is.

Mediation

Thanks to television and media, many families think that the only way to establish custody orders is to "go to court." Going to court is one way for your spouse to establish custody orders, but in many cases it's unnecessary. Letting a judge decide the fate of your divided/blended family rarely fares well for anyone involved. Although on television, the court process is often portrayed as being easy breezy, in reality, it's much more complex. When representing clients, I try my best to avoid the courtroom as much as possible. In my opinion, mediation is a better alternative.

Because my law practice also includes mediation, I'm able to compare the results of both processes. Although I'm successful achieving favorable results for my clients through litigation (the court trial process) mediation is a far more beneficial option in my opinion. I think mediation is the best way to get the best custody orders for your family because you are able to work with a professional who can help you make informed decisions, while also working with your co-parent to make sure that those decisions are best for your family.

Mediation is one of the most practical ways for parents to resolve disputes related to child custody, time-sharing, visitation, child support, and co-parenting. As no divided family is the same, no two mediators are the same and no two mediation sessions will be the same. However, typically, mediation takes place in a relaxed, yet structured atmosphere. Parents meet with the mediator to facilitate an open discussion during which they are able to confidentially communicate and discuss any issues of concern, goals, and proposed solutions.

The mediator is a neutral party. Through my mediation process, although I do not represent either party, I work carefully with the parents (sometimes stepparents included) to help them figure out what will work best for *their* blended family. I will then specifically tailor a unique agreement for the parents, which will ultimately be submitted to the Court with a request that it be made an enforceable court order.

Formal Request for Order

Unfortunately, not all parents will be able to reach an agreement regarding custody/visitation of their children. The last resort, if your spouse and the other parent aren't able to agree on issues related to their child, may be to file a motion or other request/petition for the court to make specific orders related to the custody of your stepchild. When you hear people say "I'll see you in court," this is the process they are referencing. This is the least preferred method of handling things the legal way because it can be very risky and daunting for many reasons:

Family Court Child Custody proceedings are lengthy. Compared to mediation, which is typically completed in a few sessions, family law litigation is a much lengthier process. Although temporary orders may be issued shortly after your case begins, getting permanent orders takes time – in some cases, a very long time. Exactly how long depends on your spouse, the other parent, any lawyers that are involved, and how much conflict exists.

When you litigate, no one "wins." There is no such thing as really "winning" in a litigated custody case. Asking the court to make decisions related to your family is risky because you will likely not get 100% of what you want. To get just 1/2 of what you want will likely cost you a lot of time and money required to build the case.

<u>Legal Battles are Expensive.</u> Even if your spouse doesn't hire a lawyer to represent them, you may quickly find out that there is no "cheap" way to litigate a case. Filing fees, service of process charges, court reporters, professional evaluations, and more can easily lead to thousands of dollars in costs. And once lawyers get involved on either side, that amount can easily triple.

<u>Judges don't know you.</u> When you litigate your case, you're essentially putting your family's life into the hands of a stranger. They don't know anything about your spouse, the other parent, or your stepchildren. Their decision is solely based on what is presented to them as evidence. Quite frankly, we all know that evidence presented to the court is not always the best reflection of the true circumstances or complete facts (especially if you don't have a lawyer).

<u>The best interest of your stepchild.</u> The court is going to make a determination based on what it feels is in the "best interest" of your stepchild (who they know nothing about and may never meet). Your and your spouse's definition of "best interest" and the court's idea of best interest may be on two different spectrums. The court will consider many different factors including, but not limited to:

-The child's existing living arrangements, schedule, and any potential effects significant change to such arrangements will have on the child;

-The parents' relationships with the child;

-The parents' lifestyles including abhorrent and criminal behavior or allegations of such;

-The health of the parents (both physical and mental);

-The living situation of the parents and their ability to provide for the child;

-The parents' attitudes towards the other parent's rights to the child;

-What the child wants;

-The child's age and gender.

It's important to help your spouse understand that if their case gets to the litigation stage, the court's order may not make any sense for your family. Unfortunately, once it's issued, they'll have to follow it unless your spouse and the other parent finally can agree to change it. If your spouse and the other parent can put their differences aside and really think about what's best for your stepchild before it gets to that point, everyone will probably be much better off.

<u>Judges are human.</u> Granted, they are humans with decision power not afforded to the average layperson, but...the fact still remains that, at the end of the day, they are just like you. They have a life, family, things on their "to do" list, and more. So, although it's easy to put them on a pedestal, just like you they make mistakes, have bad days, get frustrated, don't understand, and are at work. If your spouse walks into the courthouse expecting to appear before a supernatural human that can work magic...they'll be disappointed.

<u>Agreements feel better.</u> When your spouse is able to sit down and compromise, although she or he may not get everything they want, they'll at least know that what they're getting will be something that is reasonable based on your family's needs. Agreements open the door to cooperation. It's not something that is forced, but a decision your spouse had a hand in. For this reason, once they're able to reach an agreement on the bigger issues, they'll slowly be able to reach an agreement on other things and learn to work together for the benefit of your stepchild.

The fact of the matter is, when you are asking a court to make a decision that affects your life, they will not always get it right. With that in mind, if at all possible, your family should avoid getting to the point that the court has to make a decision that could change your family's life (for better or worse) for you.

Child Support

It's likely that at some point, child support will be an issue of concern for your spouse, the other parent, and even you. Specifically, who will have to pay, how much will have to be paid, and whether your income will be at risk. Although the fine points of support are much too complex to fully explain in this book, here are the need to know basics:

If obtaining child support seems to be the other parent's main focus, don't worry, you are not alone. One of the many common complaints parents (usually fathers) make is that their child's other parent seems more focused on getting child support than co-parenting or ensuring that the best interests of the child that aren't related to money are fulfilled. If this sounds familiar, there are a few things you should understand. First and foremost, before you get all wound up about child support, understand that asking for child support is a legal right for both parents.

Both parents have a duty to support their child until they turn 18 years old.

One of the most common misconceptions is that dads are <u>always</u> the parent that will have to pay child support. When a child is born, both parents have a legal duty to support that child until the child is 18 years old. Child support is not based on the gender of the parents. Both moms and dads can be ordered to pay child support.

❖ *How Child Support is Calculated*

Although both moms and dads can be ordered to pay child support, in many (not all) cases, the father is the parent that is ordered to pay. But, this is not because of his gender. Rather, it is because of the way child support is calculated. Generally, each state has a formula that is used to calculate child support according to that particular state's guidelines. This formula usually calculates the income of the parents, certain expenses, and the amount of time each parent spends with the child to determine who will pay support and the support amount. In situations where the mother has a higher income and/or a lower timeshare (the amount of time spent with their child), the mother may be ordered to pay support. However, oftentimes, fathers have a higher income than mothers. Additionally, more often than not, fathers have a lower timeshare than mothers. Consequently, fathers are commonly the parent who pays child support.

Child support is set up this way in order to ensure that the parent who assumes the most responsibility for the child will have enough financial means to adequately provide for the child. When you think about it, this approach is very logical. After all, the parent who has primary custody of the child will incur day-to-day expenses that the noncustodial parent will not incur. Specifically, the child needs daily food, clothing, shelter, lights, water, etc. Additionally, the custodial parent will incur educational, child-care, uninsured medical, and extra-curricular related expenses; not to mention travel expenses related to the same.

Many parents complain that while they don't mind paying child support to take care of their child, they are concerned about whether the receiving parent is actually using the child support to provide for the child. Many believe that the receiving parent is in fact using the support for their own personal use. Regardless of whose money is being used for what, the child's needs must be met. So, if the other parent is spending their own money to take care of the child, but uses the paying parent's money for their own personal use, the expense is essentially coming from the same source, just in the form of a reimbursement rather than a direct expense. On the other hand, if the other parent is receiving support from your spouse and not providing for the child (i.e. your stepchild is not being adequately fed, clothed, childcare isn't being paid, etc.) that's a different story. In that case, you should seek legal counsel to assist you with making sure the child support is being used to provide for the child and your child is not going without their daily necessaries.

If the child support amount ordered is more than your spouse can afford, or less than your spouse needs to care for the child, you can ask for deductions or adjustments.

Another complaint often made is that the amount of child support ordered is unaffordable. If your spouse is the paying parent, they can request that the court consider special circumstances and make specific deductions to lower the child support amount. If your spouse is the receiving parent and the child support amount is less than needed to support the child, they can ask the court to consider specific circumstances and make adjustments to raise the child support amount. Special circumstances include financial hardship, low income, extraordinary health expenses, a new baby they have with you or child support they pay for a child from a different relationship, etc. The key here is that they must specifically ask the court to consider these things. Otherwise, the court will simply use their basic information into the formula and generate a child support amount based on the state guidelines.

❖ *The Child Support Won't Change Itself*

Regardless of your circumstances, your spouse's child support benefit/obligation continues until the child turns 18 years old or one of the parent's requests modification. If your family circumstances have changed and justify an increased or decreased amount of child support (i.e. your spouse's or the other parent's income, expenses, or time with the child has changed), in order to change the support amount, they must formally request a change from the court. It's important to request modification as soon as possible after you determine that the child support amount should be changed.

❖ *Child Support and YOUR Income*

Whether your spouse's child support obligation will require you to kick in financially is a natural and reasonable concern. So here's the thing, *generally*, child support obligations specifically apply only to the child's biological/legal parents. Consequently, your income will typically not be considered. However, there are some states that require consideration of a stepparent's income in certain circumstances, specifically, when failure to consider the stepparent's income will result in detrimental harm to the children. For the most part, your greater concern should be making sure that if your spouse is ordered to pay support that he or she keeps up with that obligation, as consideration of your income when ordering child support is of no comparison to the consequences for his failure to pay support as ordered.

❖ *If Your Spouse Doesn't Pay Support*

After a formal support order is established, if your spouse doesn't pay as ordered, the consequences can be detrimental. Below is a list of just **some** of the consequences that may come into play if they don't pay child support:

1. <u>Monetary penalties added to support owed.</u>

Failure to pay support can result in owing even more support. Interest and/or penalties vary from state to state. Some states charge interest as high as 12%! Additionally, some states apply penalties.

2. <u>Negative reports to credit bureaus.</u>

If your spouse doesn't pay child support, the child support agency can report each late or non-payment to the three major credit bureaus. This can have the same impact on their credit rating as not paying their credit cards or mortgage on time. I'm sure how you can see how this can negatively affect your family's ability to make beneficial purchases such as buy a home or a car down the line.

3. <u>Bank Levies:</u>

Got money in the bank? Direct deposit? Joint account with your spouse? Banking institutions report all of the assets they hold. If your spouse doesn't pay child support, bank levies can be placed on their accounts and possibly your joint accounts. If a levy is placed on your accounts, the money can be taken before you even know it's there. Imagine expecting a paycheck for $3,000, only to find that only $500 is in your account when you get there.

4. Denial of passport

If your spouse owes more than $2,500 in back child support and you think you're going on a vacation out of the country, think again! The U.S. will not issue or renew your passport until their child support is brought current.

5. Seizure of assets.

Not only are your bank accounts at risk, any royalty checks, dividends, rental incomes, commissions, etc. your spouse is expecting can be seized also. Your real property (i.e. your home or other property you own), cash, your car or other vehicles, and even your safe deposit box contents are also at risk of seizure if your spouse doesn't pay child support. Nothing is off-limits; their unemployment, disability, or worker's compensation checks and even lottery winnings are at risk of seizure if they don't pay child support.

6. Property Liens.

Liens can also be placed on property you have or intend to sell. If this happens, if/when the property is sold, your spouse's owed child support can be taken out of the sale proceeds.

7. License Suspension.

If your spouse doesn't pay child support, any of their state-issued licenses can be suspended or withheld until they pay the support owed. Most states have a system in place that detects whether one who owes child support has or is applying for a business, professional, and/or driver's license. Yes, that means that if your spouse has or is seeking a license related to their career (doctor, teacher, lawyer, cosmetology, etc.), they may lose or be denied this license until they pay the past due support.

8. Contempt

The consequences worsen if the court finds that your spouse is able to pay support but willfully chooses not to. If this happens, your spouse may be held in contempt of court. Contempt actions can be criminal in nature; this means that your spouse could be sentenced to jail time if they fail to pay child support.

Clearly, not paying child support could put your family in a devastating position. You and your spouse could potentially lose everything you have or worse-your spouse could go to jail. Clearly, if that happens, co-parenting will be the least of your worries, so, if for some reason your spouse is unable to pay child support, they must take action to inform the court of this and request a change. Otherwise, their problems will have a domino effect and that will impact you as well. Be proactive!

The Last Resort:

So what happens when you and your spouse have honestly put in countless effort to develop a peaceful co-parenting relationship with the other parent, but your efforts have failed? What if the other parent still does not cooperate and deliberately violates a court ordered parenting plan? Sadly, there will be some parents that no matter what you do to develop a positive relationship with them, they will not cooperate and will do (or won't do) whatever they can in order to make your lives miserable. There will always be that one who just doesn't care! They don't care about their child, your spouse, you, or even themself for that matter. The good news is that if your spouse has handled their case the legal way, you will have remedies. Although the process that comes with resorting to these remedies is yet again, disruptive and frustrating for your family, nonetheless the remedies are available and you and your spouse are still better off than you would be if you had not handled things the legal way. Once you have a court order in place, you have a few options in the event that the other parent refuses to follow the court order. Below are the two most commonly used:

❖ *Enforcement*

In the event that the other parent (or your spouse) violates the court order related to child custody, many states will enable law enforcement officers to enforce the order. To do this, your spouse will need to take a certified copy of the court order to the nearest police station and file a report. Your spouse may request that an officer enforce the order. If the department is willing to enforce the order, they will go to the location where your stepchild is being withheld and speak to the parent in violation of the order and demand that they turn over the child. If they follow the officer's request, the officer will then bring your stepchild to your spouse. In the event that the other parent refuses to turn the child over, in some cases the officer will make an arrest, but in most, the officer will usually make a police report so that your spouse may file a court action for enforcement/contempt.

❖ *Contempt*

A contempt action may be filed if your spouse or the other parent willfully violates the child custody, child support, or any other court order. Contempt actions are criminal in nature and for the most part are considered misdemeanors, punishable by up to six months in county jail and/or a fine up to $1,000.

These are obviously measures that hopefully your spouse will not be forced to make, but it is imperative that your spouse knows of their rights and duties as a parent, and be ready and willing to utilize all options available to ensure the welfare and safety of your stepchild.

Stepparent adoption

If the other parent is a true deadbeat and has shown no interest in being in your stepchild's life and you have fully assumed all parental responsibilities, you may want to consider discussing the possibility of a stepparent adoption with your spouse. Generally, to obtain a stepparent adoption, your spouse and the child's other biological parent (the deadbeat) will have to give their consent. Since they do not have an interest in parenting and especially do not have an interest in financially supporting your stepchild, you may be able to obtain this consent without dispute. After all, this is one of the only ways they can give up their parental rights and thereby be relieved of their financial obligation to support the child. If your spouse discusses this option with them and they do not agree, don't worry, there's still hope. If a parent has abandoned their child (i.e., has deliberately been absent or failed to provide financial support), especially if it's been one year or more, the court may be able to grant the step-parent adoption even if the other parent doesn't agree. The chances are even better if you have stepped into the parenting role as your stepchild's other parent, and have done so for an extended period of time. Whether the adoption will be granted is based upon what is in the best interest of your stepchild. If you are dealing with a deadbeat, I'm certain you and your spouse can make a pretty good argument that having you, a loving step-parent adopt them in place of the other parent who, based on their actions, does not want parental responsibility, is in your child's best interest.

Stepparent rights

One of the most devastating issues that blended families face, specifically you as the stepparent, is the reality that when it all comes down to it, the law provides you with very little right to your stepchildren absent a legal stepparent adoption. While surely you are expected to care for your stepchildren and assume full responsibility for them when they are in your care (similar to the care you'd be required to give any other minor relative or visitor you're entrusted with), that's pretty much the extent of your legal right and responsibility.

The good news is, so long as you and your spouse are married and they give authority to you to be involved in certain aspects of your stepchild's life even against the other parent's objection:

❖ *Medical Treatment*

Generally, stepparents do not have rights to make decisions related to their stepchild's medical care. Of course an exception to this is when you are acting as your stepchild's primary caretaker in your spouse's absence. To be on the safe side, it's a good idea to have your spouse sign a consent form that authorizes medical providers to care for your child in the event of an emergency or when a visit to the doctor is otherwise necessary.

❖ Education

As a stepparent, you will have the right to make minor education decisions related to your stepchild as well as review and receive a copy of their school records. Pursuant to The Family Educational Rights and Privacy Act (FERPA), parents have the right to inspect and review their child's school records. Stepparents are included in the definition of "parent" so long as the parent lives with the biological parent and stepchild at least part of the time. This means that even if the other parent objects to your involvement in your stepchild's education, your spouse can authorize your involvement and can authorize you to receive communications and other information related to your stepchild's education without the other parent's consent.

❖ If You and Your Spouse Divorce

Unfortunately, when it comes to a stepparent's rights after divorce, things become a lot more complicated. Technically, in a divorce, the only parent with legal rights to the stepchildren are the biological parents. To stepparents, this is disappointing because essentially this means that in the event of dissolution of your marriage, you could easily be stripped of your relationship with your stepchild despite the relationship and bond you may have developed with them over the years. Many stepparents put in a lot of time, energy, and effort bonding with their stepchildren, developing unconditional love for them and want to continue that relationship with them irrespective of their divorce.

Obviously this will not be an issue if their stepchildren are adults. However, in the case where their stepchildren are minors, accomplishing this can become problematic, as there aren't any laws set in stone that guarantee a stepparent's continued right to a relationship with their stepchild. In fact, the Supreme Court has maintained that a child's parents have a "fundamental right to make decisions concerning the care, custody, and control of their children." - including who has the right to have access and make decisions related to their children. Consequently, this means that if you and your spouse divorce, unless you are in agreement that you can exercise custody or visitation of that child, depending on your state, you may have little recourse in establishing said visitation.

The good news is that many states will allow you to petition for visitation and will make a determination based on what the court deems is in the best interest of the child. You would also have the same option to petition the court for custody or visitation in the event that your spouse were to pass away. Unfortunately the mere fact that you are the child's stepparent is not enough to warrant an order for custody or visitation. You will likely have to prove that you not only had a substantial role in your stepchild's life, but also that your continued relationship would be in your stepchild's best interest.

V.

THE BUSINESS OF CO-PARENTING

The business of co-parenting is just like any other business; it takes genuine commitment, hard work, and constant, conscious efforts. Although it may require major adjustments in the way you have been dealing with your blended family, once you take full responsibility for your mindset and your actions, and help your spouse do the same (regardless of what the other parent is doing), you will become the master of your blended family's future and live in harmony.

Just like businesses have bylaws to abide by, so should your blended family. There are several things that if implemented, can prevent, lessen, and even destroy drama in your family. Although all blended families are different, these general blended family "business" rules can be applied to all and expanded upon as you see fit:

Blended Family Bylaws

❖ *Blended Family Language*

As blended families, we already face an uphill battle to get to a point that we feel like a solid family unit. The way you speak to and of your blended family is just one of the things that impacts the dynamic of your relationships. *Think about it:* when someone's words are encouraging, we feel good. When someone speaks well of us, it makes us happy. The same goes for your family. If you speak to and of your family as though you are unified, at some point you will likely be. If you speak of your family like you're divided, that's how you'll remain.

❖ *"Baby Mamas and Baby Daddies"*

Naturally, you may refer to the other parent as your spouse's "baby daddy" or "baby mama." Unless your family is on a drama-filled reality tv show (or unless that's your goal), you should stop referring to the other parent in this manner.

Believe it or not, we speak our worlds into existence. If all you want for your spouse is a "baby daddy/mama," then carry on referring to them as such. However, if it's your desire to have a positive and cooperative co-parent, you should start speaking that over them. That is your stepchild's other parent, your co-parenting partner. You are your child's stepparent. Respect and refer to each other as such.

❖ *"The Steps"*

Yes, we know that a "stepfamily" is one in which one or both spouses have children from another relationship. But, when families blend, why is there a need to distinguish? Everyone in the family knows who the "mom", "dad", and "step" parents are, there's really no need to remind each other every day. To me, referring to your family as a "step" anything only adds an element of separation. The only time I refer to my stepson as my "stepson" is if I'm providing a detailed explanation that requires it (such as this book). When I introduce him to someone, I refer to him as my son. When I speak of him, I always say "I have three children", not "I have two of my own and one stepchild." We are one family unit, regardless of our bloodline, and there's no reason for us to feel otherwise.

It was no different for my stepson. Before we decided that "step" was just not a word we would use in our family, I could see the discomfort in his demeanor when he would introduce or refer to me as his "stepmom." Now, he comfortably refers to me as his mom (and clarifies if necessary), bonus mom, or mom #2. This decreases the need for him to provide an explanation about our relationship to those who don't really need it. The same goes for my stepson's mom. When she refers to me, she refers to me as his other mom and when we talk about our son, we refer to him as that: "OUR" son.

If you have to distinguish between your biological and marital relationship, try using "bonus child", "bonus mom", or "bonus dad" instead of "step." Step feels more like a burden or inconvenience, while "bonus" feels more like an advantage, something special, something more solid.

❖ *Disparaging Remarks*

Again, the words you speak regarding your blended family are instrumental in the dynamic of your relationships. This includes not only the words you use to refer to your blended family members, but also the words you use to describe them. The mantra "If you don't have anything nice to say, don't say anything at all" is best applied here.

Disparaging remarks are those words that are derogatory, disapproving, or critical. You know, the ones you may speak (or are tempted to speak) on your and the other parent's worst day. The words you want to say about them, but you shouldn't say out loud. The words that if your stepchild were to hear them, would make them uncomfortable, or worse - hurt them. Think about it like this: Regardless of how you feel about the other parent, the fact remains that he or she is still their parent. They are your spouse's ex, but not your stepchild's ex. Your spouse's relationship with them may be over, but their relationship with your stepchild will remain forever. Considering this, it's imperative that neither you nor your spouse be the cause of any dysfunction in their relationship.

By making negative comments about the other parent to your stepchild, in their presence, or within their hearing distance, you can potentially cause them to feel negatively about them. You in essence may be transferring your own personal emotions and opinions to them. The same goes for your friends and family; their negative opinions about the other parent are off limits in the presence of your stepchildren. Children repeat what they hear grown-ups say, they learn what we teach them. What are you and your spouse teaching them about their other parent? Your negative perceptions of them may be correct. However, it's not your job to ruin their independent perception of them.

The reality is, if they're really as "bad" as you think, you won't have to say one word to your child about it; he/she will learn everything they need to know about them on their own, based on their actions and interactions with them.

Even after the intense custody battle and drama our blended family experienced, we have all managed to refrain from discussing those negative experiences or feelings with or around our child. In fact, though he was definitely affected by our situation, it happened so long ago and we've secluded him from it so much that he neither remembers nor knows that we went through all of the things we did; in his mind, we've always had a good relationship. This has been paramount in our son's peace and has allowed him to develop and maintain positive relationships with all of us comfortably.

❖ *Check Your Village*

Ever heard the quote: "It takes a village to raise a child?" This quote speaks volumes. In order for children to thrive and develop into the wonderful human beings they have the potential to become, they need positive, supportive, influential people in their lives to give them direction and teach them core values of life. The same applies to your blended family relationships. In order to get to a place of peace and cooperation with the other parent, you must be surrounded by people who support this goal. There's nothing worse than someone who has good intentions when it comes to doing something positive, yet is surrounded by naysayers and people with negative attitudes whose energy transfers to them.

I remember there was a lady who followed me on social media and was interested in one of my resources/programs for divided/blended families. She tagged her friend in the comments of one of my promotional posts indicating that she was thinking of participating in my program because she was tired of the drama with her child's father. Rather than supporting her, her "friend" responded in the comments, basically saying "you don't need this, you do just fine being both mom and dad for your child." This was so disappointing to me: here you had a young lady who acknowledged the fact that she was struggling to build a positive relationship with her child's father and was considering getting help to change her situation. Yet, the one friend that she may have called on for sound advice basically told her "you don't need to change anything, your child is just fine without their dad." This is the perfect example of needing to check your village.

Ever heard the saying "show me who your closest friends are and I'll show you your future"? Yet another mantra that applies to divided/blended families. If your circle consists of a bunch of no good, "baby daddies" whose children don't have relationships with them, naturally you may take on the same attitude. However, if you're surrounded by parents who are constantly on a mission to create better for their children, then you will naturally be inspired to strive for the same. It's hard to aim for progress when no one around you is progressing. It's hard to be optimistic about your blended family if everyone around you is negative. It's hard to build a life of greatness for your stepchild, if everyone around you is content with mediocrity. So, take a moment, think about the top five people who you call on regularly for friendship and really think about the kind of energy they give out. Are they shining light into your life? Or are they more often consumed with darkness. If you want to change your situation, you have to check your village, and adjust as necessary.

❖ *The 5 c's Of Co-Parenting*

The business of co-parenting requires what I like to call **The 5 C's of Co-Parenting:**

1) Communication;

2) Compromise;

3) Conflict Prevention;

4) Consideration; and

5) Cooperation.

Communication

Communication is one of the most important aspects of ANY relationship. But it is especially important when co-parenting. Even if you believe that certain things are common sense and you should not have to *literally* communicate those things, it is in the best interest of all parties involved that you clearly communicate your thoughts whenever possible. No two people think alike. For example, just because it makes sense to me that my four-year-old should not be allowed to play outside around the neighborhood without adult supervision, does not mean that others believe the same.

In fact, I have a neighbor whose two and three-year-old children run all around the neighborhood by themselves. Again, just because it makes sense to *me* that smoking in the presence of your children is not only inappropriate, but also a health risk, I have met people who smoke around their children on a daily basis and do not give it a second thought.

The point is, it is not reasonable to assume that others think and do exactly as you. Nor can you always expect people to know your expectations. Most of us cannot read minds (although some claim to have this power). If you want someone to know something, you have to communicate that something - even if you believe they should know without you telling them. It is better to communicate too much (effectively) than too little. Now, the subject of how to effectively communicate is literally a completely independent topic for another book. However, here are some very basic tips to keep in mind when communicating with the other parent:

Remain cool, calm, collected, and respectful - Keep your emotions out of it. In the heat of the moment, follow the 3-hour rule; The 3-hour rule keeps you from communicating at the height of emotion. If you find yourself in the heat of the moment, wait 3 hours before communicating with the other parent. This tip prevents many co-parents from saying or doing something they will later regret. If you are angry, upset, frustrated, or just annoyed, try to wait until you have cooled off. Once you have cooled off, think of a tactful way to communicate your position to them and encourage your spouse to do the same. Talk *to* them, not *down* to them. Having a condescending tone will only make matters worse. Regardless of how you feel, disrespect is a no-no. No yelling, no profanity allowed. A good approach is to follow the motto "If you don't have anything nice to say, don't say anything at all." While it's okay and oftentimes necessary to explain your position, whether it be an agreement or disagreement, you must always do so respectfully. This goes for both you and your spouse.

<u>Be clear</u> - Say what you mean, mean what you say. Most of us aren't mind readers. Never assume that the other parent "knows" what you want or need from them and that you are on the same page. You need to be clear in your expectations and make sure that they understand them.

Communicate in writing as much as possible - When it comes to communication related to your stepchild, it's best to communicate in writing as much as possible. If you or your spouse have an important conversation with the other parent, send a follow up email to confirm the conversation to ensure you are in agreement. Not only does this avoid confusion about what exactly was said, but it also creates a record for you to use in the future if necessary. However, when communicating in writing, try to be mindful of your tone and your choice of words, as unlike verbal communication, you can't take back a text message or email that has been sent.

Compromise

Whenever practical, encourage compromise. The bottom line is both parents cannot always get what they want when it comes to decisions concerning their child. Therefore, while your spouse may *know* what's best, you may have to remind them that there are two parents, both whose opinions matter. The best way to prevent potential problems due to disagreement is to understand the importance of compromise. Express the importance of carefully picking battles - everything is not worth the fight. Before making a fuss about an issue, make sure

117

that you have had ample opportunity to clearly view the full picture. You have to decide what's important to fight over, and what you are willing to compromise on. Carefully consider the other parent's position. Does any of it make sense? Will going with their suggestion hurt your situation? Or is their simply a disagreement because it's not what you or your spouse had in mind? Insisting that things always go your way, specifically without being reasonable, is not co-parenting and will likely lead to more stress and chaos in the long run.

Conflict Prevention

I cannot stress enough the importance of being proactive. Your spouse and the other parent should discuss issues that may come up later such as religion, education, traveling out of the country, holidays, vacation, who is allowed to babysit your stepchild, etc. It's important that they establish as many agreements as possible regarding your stepchild while they are on good terms. It's even more important that your spouse formalize the agreements and obtain court orders. Another good idea is to put a system in place that will prevent deadlock such as "rock, paper, scissors," drawing out of a hat, flipping a coin, or asking a third, neutral party to make the final decision in the event that your spouse is unable to agree on an issue. This may sound trivial now, but believe me, it may solve problems that are far from trivial when in the heat of the moment.

Consideration

Because there are two (or more) parents and one child (or several children), it's important to always have consideration for each other. You must be considerate of each other's time, schedule, feelings, and relationship with your stepchild. Before making major decisions related to your stepchild, make sure you and/or your spouse discuss them with the other parent so they can give their input. Before making plans with your stepchild that may interfere with the other parent's custodial time, discuss your proposed plans with them and a possible way to make up that missed time if they want. Be considerate of their feelings.

Always remain considerate of your stepchild's relationship with the other parent. Encourage your stepchild to continue to develop the bond with them. In spite of how you or your spouse feel about the other parent, do not say or do things that will make your stepchild uncomfortable about having a relationship with them and don't allow others to either. If the other parent is a deadbeat, it's unnecessary for you to remind your stepchild of this. If the other parent isn't parenting up to your standards, that's not your stepchild's business; that is between you, your spouse, and the other parent. Most importantly, do not argue with the other parent in front of your stepchild. Your disagreements are private matters to be discussed between the adults only. The last thing you need is for your stepchild to develop ill feelings for you, your spouse, or the other parent due to your comments and actions. This may be very hard to do, but it is crucially important. Always be the bigger person.

Cooperation

Co-parenting is all about teamwork. The business of co-parenting will be considerably more successful if you, your spouse, and your child's other parent support one another. This means that all of you should attempt to, at a minimum, have similar parenting ideals and make sure that your stepchild understands that you are working together for their benefit. If you have an issue with your stepchild, make an effort to incorporate the other parent into your discipline method, even if that just means making a phone call to them in front of your stepchild and informing them about the problem. If for one reason or another the other parent cannot keep their scheduled visitation, help out if you are able to; switch days with them, keep your stepchild an extra day or two, and depend on them to do the same for you.

When it comes to your stepchild's education and extracurricular activities, make sure that all of you are involved as much as possible. Attend parent-teacher conferences and parent council meetings together. When you send correspondence to your stepchild's school, make sure that both household's names are signed on the correspondence whenever practical so that the school is aware that both parents' households are involved. Cheer your stepchild on together at events. It may seem awkward at first, but you'll get used to it and it will put your stepchild at ease. Remember at the beginning of this book when I said I have personal experience? Trust me, I do. My husband and I have attended numerous parent-teacher conferences with my stepson's mother and most recently, his step-father has also attended. As a result, the teacher and other administrators at his school recognized that my stepson has a strong support system. We also attend sports events, award assemblies, and occasionally even birthday parties for my stepson together. Even if we don't sit together the entire time, we acknowledge one another, and interact peacefully. From the outside looking in, you are not able to tell that any ill feelings ever existed between our two homes, and believe me, at one point there was some extreme illness happening. While initially all of this may have been a bit awkward, ultimately, the benefits outweighed the awkwardness as our divided/blended family has progressed and, as a result, our family lives in peace.

I know the concept of the business of co-parenting may seem like a lot of work, especially if you have to work hard in an effort to influence the other parent to get on the same page, set aside the drama, and work with you and your spouse in considering the best interests of your stepchild. But, although it is a process that requires a lot of consideration, strategy, and action on your behalf, tackling the issues discussed in this book and taking action will ultimately pay off. Regardless of what the other parent does or does not do, your blended family deserves to live in peace. This means that in order to achieve this peace, you have to step out of your comfort zone and take control as the responsible investor in your blended family. Much of the success of your co-parenting relationship depends largely on you and your spouse. Keep in mind that even the simplest decisions you make may detrimentally affect your child both now and later. The good news is, by making smart, selfless decisions now, your child has a greater chance of having a bright future. And that's the business of co-parenting.

MEET MERISSA V. GRAYSON

Also known as "America's Blended Family Expert," Merissa V. Grayson is a dynamic and driven Lawyer, Author, Mediator and Co-Parenting + Blended Family Advocate.

Merissa's background stems not only from her professional experience as a Child Custody & Family Law Attorney, but also from her experience as a Wife and Stepmother who has personally disentangled the difficult challenges that often come with the territory of divided & blended family living.

Merissa has dedicated her life to helping families around the country tackle similar challenges by truly walking them through positive transformations to help them gain the lifestyle and peace of mind they deserve.

www.ingramcontent.com/pod-product-compliance
Lightning Source LLC
LaVergne TN
LVHW041322080426
835513LV00008B/549